The Scarecrow Author Bibliographies

1. *John Steinbeck: A Concise Bibliography (1930-1965)*, by Tetsumaro Hayashi. 1967.

2. *A Bibliography of Joseph Conrad*, by Theodore G. Ehrsam. 1969.

3. *Arthur Miller Criticism (1930-1967)*, by Tetsumaro Hayashi. 1969.

4. *A Bibliography of the Works of Katherine Anne Porter and of the Criticism of the Works* . . . by Louise Waldrip and Shirley Anne Bauer. 1969.

5. *Freneau's Published Prose: A Bibliography*, by Philip M. Marsh. 1970.

6. *Robert Greene Criticism. A Comprehensive Bibliography*, by Tetsumaro Hayashi. 1971.

7. *Benjamin Disraeli*, by R. W. Stewart. 1972.

8. *John Berryman: A Checklist*, by Richard W. Kelly. 1972.

9. *William Dean Howells: A Bibliography*, by Vito J. Brenni. 1973.

10. *Jean Anouilh: An Annotated Bibliography*, by Kathleen White Kelly. 1973.

11. *E. M. Forster: An Annotated Bibliography of Secondary Materials*, by Alfred Borrello. 1973.

12. *The Marquis de Sade: A Bibliography*, by E. Pierre Chanover. 1973.

13. *Alain Robbe-Grillet: An Annotated Bibliography of Critical Studies, 1953-1972*, by Dale Watson Fraizer. 1973.

E. M. FORSTER

An Annotated Bibliography of Secondary Materials

by

ALFRED BORRELLO

The Scarecrow Author Bibliographies, No. 11

The Scarecrow Press, Inc.
Metuchen, N. J.   1973

c C

Library of Congress Cataloging in Publication Data

Borrello, Alfred.
   E. M. Forster: an annotated bibliography of
secondary materials.

   (The Scarecrow author bibliographies, no. 11)
   1. Forster, Edward Morgan, 1879-1970--Bibliography.
I. Title.
Z8309.3.B67   016.823'9'12   73-7790
ISBN 0-8108-0668-1

To

J. M. J.

and

Denise and Philip Borrello

as I

promised

CONTENTS

PREFACE

Several years before the death of E. M. Forster in 1970, I conceived of a project--a trilogy of volumes--which would offer the general reader, the student, and the scholar help in understanding the contribution of a writer whom many consider one of the major novelists of this century. This volume represents the capstone of that project.

It is the first major Forsterian bibliography of secondary materials, annotated or otherwise, to appear in print. There do exist, however, two other attempts to compile bibliographies of some substance; chiefly the efforts published regularly in English Literature in Transition, and the shorter, non-annotated checklist in Modern Fiction Studies, which are noted in their proper places in this work. Neither of these efforts, nevertheless, equals the comprehensiveness of this volume.

As I pursued my research for this work, I could not help but mark that much of what has been written about Forster and his contribution is not genuinely worthy of collection. However, for the sake of a certain level of completeness, the reader will find the dross and, what little there is of it, the gold of the commentary. That commentary almost invariably takes one of two directions. It sometimes turns to emotional, non-critical "appreciations" of Forster--a position epitomized by Rose Macaulay's early book-length study. The predominating direction, however, is that which uses Forster's work as support for the liberal-humanist tradition. The latter is the posture reflected in Lionel Trilling's very influential work.

It is not difficult to understand how these two directions arose. It seems impossible for critics and scholars to approach Forster's materials from a balanced middle-ground. They either love his work or abhor it. They see it as a support for their private and comfortable beliefs, or they understand it as an attack on all they hold dear and, therefore, to be condemned. That Rose Macaulay wrote of Forster as she did is understandable. She speaks more of the man than of his art, and this is logical; she was his friend. But even those commentators who did not know him personally tend to speak of the man more than of his work. Since the publication of A Passage to India in 1924, Forster, the man, began to be metamorphosed into Forster, the symbol. He was more than a little bewildered by all of the adulation which was his in this period. He remarked once of how he was a bit "tired" of his notoriety and of the novel that many consider his masterpiece. Perhaps out of pique, he would always respond that The Longest Journey, the least successful of his novels, was his favorite. Nevertheless, the symbol grew. Through his reviews, his minor essays, and eventually his two collections of these minor writings, he began to take on all the aspects of the defender of liberalism in a world becoming more and more illiberal.

The novels being never far from propaganda, and the short stories and minor articles offering almost nothing but propaganda, Forster's works readily lent themselves as source materials for those who would mine them for such purposes. Coupled with this possibility was the ever growing respect--in the United States, reverence approaching worship--with which he was regarded. It is no wonder that Trilling's position was capable of rousing armies of imitators. Further, it is interesting to note that the so-called "Forster revival," to which we owe so much of the commentary, came only in the post-war years when colleges, particularly in the United States, expanded at an unprecedented pace; and along with this expansion came the ever increasing necessity for English faculties to "publish or perish." Forster's materials, because of their essential ambiguities and their heavy use of symbols, provide a gold mine for those in need of a published article or, in some instances, as the reader will see when he looks within this volume, a dissertation or a book. Much of the ephemera listed in this bibliography originated in this hectic period. Indeed, the number of articles produced in the last twenty years is more than twice the number published when Forster was at the height of his productive years.

Lest the reader believe that no other materials are noted here except those of an "appreciative" or propagandistic nature, I must point out that there is yet another, albeit a smaller voice in Forster criticism. These commentaries examine his writings not so much for philosophical reflections of their creators' private beliefs, but for the art which Forster practiced. It is hoped that my bibliography will encourage this "direction," if only by pointing out the surfeit of materials which reflect the first two positions.

Unhappily, since his death, yet another viewpoint seems to be evolving which appears to be as controlling of Forster criticism as those of Macaulay and Trilling. Almost from the moment of Forster's death, friends whom he cherished in life, raced into print to reveal the dark corners of his private life which he had successfully concealed from the general public. It is ironic that he who thought so highly of friendship should have his reputation suffer so in the hands of those very friends whom he revered. Further, an awful novel--awful as art--Maurice, was published posthumously. Its publication will certainly lead to the reevaluation of all of his work. The five novels he chose to publish in his lifetime will now be scrutinized for homosexual implications. One shudders to think what will be made of the Fielding-Aziz friendship in A Passage to India! Let us hope that in some way the art he produced will not drown in this search for sensationalism.

There is, however, a happy side to all of this. In September 1972, Edward Arnold published a collection of Forster's short stories (The Life to Come), all but one of which have never been published. The collection carries an introduction which will finally put an end to the flood of articles speculating on why Forster never wrote fiction after 1924. Those of us who enjoy the one masterpiece and the four near misses he has produced will be eternally grateful.

Now, at the end of a project which took some five years to complete, I cannot close this preface without thanking those responsible for the appearance of this and the other three volumes. Chiefly my thanks go to Thomas Hurley whose conversations with me on Forster gave rise to the project; to the patient librarians of the New York Public Library; the libraries of St. John's University and Columbia University, who never seemed discouraged by yet another question; and to my publisher, who saw the value of this series.

Alfred Borrello

Brooklyn, New York
December, 1972.

INTRODUCTION

This is the third and last of three volumes of basic
tools of reference for the student, scholar, and general
reader interested in the work of E. M. Forster. The first
of these volumes, already published, An E. M. Forster Dic-
tionary, was created in the tradition of the Dickens and
Faulkner dictionaries but is more uniform and more inclus-
ive. It contains summaries of his fiction and non-fiction accompanied by full publication data. In addition, it lists and
describes all of his characters, key geographical locations,
sites, hotels, etc. The second volume, also now published,
An E. M. Forster Glossary, is an alphabetical listing of
Forster's allusions, drawn from his novels, short stories,
and essays. The listing includes such disparate items as
allusions to writers and writing, historic personages,
mythology, music and musicians, art and artists, historical
events, etc. All of these are explained and cross-referenced.
Further, an attempt has been made to trace the originals of
many of his fictional characters. Quotations and their sour-
ces are also given as well as literal translations of passages
in foreign languages.

This volume is a listing and annotation of a representative body of commentary upon Forster and his works up to
and including the year of his death, 1970. It is by far the
most comprehensive bibliography, annotated or otherwise, to
be published to date. It includes many items from outside
of Great Britain and the United States, but these items cannot be considered exhaustive. This listing includes, along
with book and pamphlet-length studies, notations of the
dramatizations of his work and reviews of their performances;
items of a biographical nature--in the form of interviews
published in periodicals and news items from the London
Times and the New York Times, but from no other newspapers since these would tend to be unnecessarily repetitious;
doctoral dissertations, published or otherwise, have also
been listed, but undergraduate papers and masters' theses,
have been excluded. Newspaper and periodical reviews of
Forster's books have been annotated. It seemed wise to go
beyond the New York Times and the London Times for these,

but reviews from continental newspapers, because they are generally unavailable, have been excluded. Annotations of references to Forster in general literary histories are given, but these are representative, not exhaustive. References to his work in college and high school texts are generally omitted unless they are readily available in public and school libraries. In general, reprints of his short stories are noted if they are accompanied by commentary of some length. Bibliographies are included, generally with no annotation except in those instances in which the titles do not reveal the contents.

A word must be said about the nature of the annotations offered. Whenever possible, they give the central thesis of the work. All too many articles, unhappily, have no central focus. In these instances, a summary of the contents is noted. Book and pamphlet-length studies are annotated chapter by chapter. There are several items for which the reader will find no annotation. They are items which were not available.

There are several avenues of access to the information offered in this bibliography not the least significant of which are the various indexes, but browsing is not to be discounted. Herein lie the history and nature of Forster's public and critical popularity from year to year. The curious will discover, all too readily, that his popularity was not large and that he was not always well received.

The entries are listed as simply as possible and cross-referenced when necessary. In several instances, notably in the case of books, reprints and new editions are indicated. They are listed year by year and alphabetically by author within each year. When no author is given, the entry is alphabetized by title. In entries for periodicals, Roman numbers indicate the volume. This is followed by the date and the page numbers. Newspaper entries offer the date, page numbers, and when necessary the number of the section and column. In annotations of books and pamphlets, chapters are indicated by Roman numbers.

LIST OF ABBREVIATIONS USED

AH	Abinger Harvest
Aspects	Aspects of the Novel
Celest	The Celestial Omnibus and Other Stories
Collect	The Collected Tales
EMF	E. M. Forster
Eternal	The Eternal Moment and Other Stories
GLD	Goldsworthy Lowes Dickinson
Hill	The Hill of Devi
LJ	The Longest Journey
MT	Marianne Thornton: A Domestic Biography
PI	A Passage to India
PP	Pharos and Pharillon
RWV	A Room with a View
Story	"The Story of the Siren"
Two	Two Cheers for Democracy
VW	Virginia Woolf
WAFT	Where Angels Fear to Tread

ANNOTATED BIBLIOGRAPHY

1907

1. "The Longest Journey" (review), Bookman (London), XXXII (June 1907), 109.
   The book is "clever, glamourous and arresting" and full of "uncommon persons." EMF fails, however, in making them "continually abnormal." Consequently, "his clever book is 'starred' with crudities and violence."

2. "Mr. E. M. Forster," Bookman (London), XXXII (June 1907), 81-82.
   EMF is truly a "new" author. LJ, in breadth of design and treatment, and in the "subtle charm" of its style, touches a higher level than was reached by WAFT. The author does "not hamper himself with any artistic formula." Some of his opinions of men and things are "healthily irritating." He has "wit and humour, and a good gift of irony."

1910

3. "Howards End" (review), Athenaeum, CXXXVI (3 Dec 1910), 696.
   The novel assures EMF a "place amongst the handful of living writers who count." Its defects are that his characters are "points of view" rather than people and that the "moral" is wrong, i.e. that which is bad ought to be loved.

4. "Howards End" (review), Saturday Review (London), CX (26 Nov 1910), 688.
   The novel is "too big to be either set aside or grappled to our souls at once; it will have to find its level after repeated regustation."

5. "Howards End" (review), Spectator (London), CV (5 Nov

1910), 757.
"Surprise" is the essence of EMF's method. His
story may be roughly described as "a set of free variations
on the old theme of amantium viae. " The book has "vivid
characterization and a happy command of dialogue. "

1911

6. "Howards End" (review), Current Literature, L (April
    1911), 454.
        The reviewer is a "trifle puzzled and a trifle bored"
by the laudatory reviews and enthusiasm which have greeted
the novel.

7. "Howards End" (review), Independent, LXX (27 April
    1911), 903.
        A "very original book. " EMF has a "rare mastery
of dialog, of character drawing, and of the action and reaction of character upon circumstance. "

8. " 'Howards End' by EMF. A Novel That Suggests the
    Work of Galsworthy but Lacks the Galsworthian Strength, "
    New York Times Book Review, XVI (19 Feb. 1911), 94.
        EMF has not as yet arrived at any positive convic-
tions as a "social philosopher. " Nevertheless, Howards End
is fashioned in the likeness of the sociological-psychological
novel.   The three families are "evidently designed to epito-
mize three distinct social strata. "   Among its "multiplicity
of motifs" the reader will recognize the "shadowy counter-
parts" of certain themes treated "with greater vigor by
Galsworthy in The Country House, The Man of Property, Fra-
ternity, and by 'Miss Sinclair. ' " EMF's metier is comedy. He
"evinces neither power nor inclination to come to grips with
any vital problem. "

9. "Like Father, Like Son: Their Candid, Innocent Serious-
    ness in 'RWV', " New York Times Book Review, XVI
    (30 July 1911), 472.
        EMF has a "very pretty comedy gift obscured by a
somewhat foggy social philosophy. " The quality of his
"mirth" shows the influence of Meredith but "happily" he is
not "imitative. "

10. "The New Books" (review of RWV), Outlook, LXXXXVIII
    (10 June 1911), 310.
        RWV has a "rare quality" which "rivets one's at-
tention from the very first" and is filled with "witty bits of

description. "

11. "Some Women on Marriage" (review of HE), Review of
    Reviews, XXXXIII (June 1911), 759-760.
        HE is the story of an "intellectually honest woman"
who marries a Philistine and makes the best of him. She
lives in the "possession of a happy philosophy which she expressed in some very brilliant, witty sentences. "

1920

12. Boynton, H. W. "Good Novels of Several Kinds, "
    Bookman, LI (May 1920), 342.
        A review of WAFT. The novel should appeal to
those who welcome an "unfamiliar touch or flavor." The character Gino "is worth studying as a hint toward the comprehension of our Italian cousin, whether the peanut man on the
corner, or a D'Annunzio. "

13. "Tears and Laughter, " New York Times Book Review,
    (11 April 1920), 168.
        A review of WAFT. A book "quite out of the
ordinary, " it is a "blending of comedy and tragedy ... skill-
fully ... developed. "

14. "Where Angels Fear to Tread" (review), Booklist,
    XVII (Oct 1920), 32.
        "An odd and delightful piece of work. "

15. "Where Angels Fear to Tread" (review), Bookman, LII
    (Oct 1920), 175.
        EMF "has the ability to scoff at life and yet enjoy it
fully at the same time. " The "characters of the peasantry
... are exceptionally well drawn. " The novel is, above all,
"human. "

16. "Where Angels Fear to Tread" (review), Dial, LXVIII
    (May 1920), 665.
        The novel is "trite only in title. " It contains somer-
saults of motive and swift satire. "

17. "Where Angels Fear to Tread: Novel by E. M.
    Forster Contrasting English and Italian Manners but with
    Emotional Ending, " Springfield Republican, Magazine and
    Auto Section, (21 March 1920), 11A.
        EMF is "an artist of distinction. " The novel "has
the subtle comprehension, the subdued irony, the charm of

temperament and the delicacy of style that have been found in all of his books; and it presents that same merger of comedy and tragedy which was attempted in HE."

1921

18. "Howards End" (review), Dial, LXXI (Oct 1921), 483.
    The novel is a reprint new to the United States. In it, EMF shows a "keenness of perception of small encounters." His characters are "nervous, sensitive, alive." He fails, however, in his "efforts at symbolism" and his "spiritual values blur."

19. "Howards End (review), New Republic, XXVI (20 April
    1921), 246.
    Few modern writers have revealed "so robust a sense of the elusive and intangible." This is so because EMF "has realized the importance of relating even the most tentative conclusion about life as firmly as possible to the whole of life."

20. Mais, Stuart Petre Brodie. Why We Should Read.
    London: Grant Richards, 1921. pp. 152-156.
    Though EMF has written "a number of novels" he is "remembered by one [HE] and that is a decade old." He has greater interest in classical myths "rather than us." He is a "scholar" with "a good deal of the poet in him." HE is read for its "unexpectedness, its elliptic talk, which so exactly hits off the characters he creates, for its manifestation of the comic spirit."

21. "Recent Books in Review," Bookman, LIV (Oct 1921),
    172-173.
    A review of HE. "We unconditionally surrendered to its charm of diction, its inimitable humor, and its generous humanity."

22. "Shorter Notices," Freeman, III (13 July 1921), 431.
    A review of HE. The novel has a story "held together by a logical and lucid mind." EMF weaves an "attractive narrative, touched with irony and illuminated by his imaginative grasp of motive and character."

1922

23. Dutton, George B. "Howards End Shows up Disjointed
    Living, " Springfield Republican, Magazine, Auto and
    Theater Section, (1 Jan 1922), 11A.
        A review of HE. The novel is "one of the most ar-
    resting of recent novels though not 'recent. ' " It is a work
    of "such unusual flavor that one is glad to have it brought to
    the attention of Americans. " In a way, the inscription "only
    connect" is the "theme of the novel. " The "variations upon
    the theme unfold as in a symphony with exquisite naturalness. "

24. Evans, Powys. "Portrait, " London Mercury, VII (Dec
    1922), 131.
        A drawing of EMF by Powys Evans.

25. Goodall, Edyth. "Mr. E. M. Forster's Books, " Times
    (London), (16 June 1922), 16, col. 3, bottom.
        A letter indicating the correspondent's "deepest debt"
    to EMF for his HE because of its "lasting beauty" and the
    fact that it is "a constant surprise. "

26. Johnson, Richard Brimley. Some Contemporary Novel-
    ists, (Men). London: Parsons, 1922. pp. 173-181.
        There is much, especially in HE, in EMF which
    reminds us of Henry James. There follows a comparison of
    James's manner with that of EMF. "They do not undress
    their characters, etc. " The subject matter of WAFT might
    have been chosen by any of his contemporaries. LJ is a
    more obvious and continuous struggle between "the vision"
    and what EMF calls "the teacup of experience. " Johnson
    takes issue with those who say that EMF's reputation will
    rest upon Celest.

27. "The Longest Journey, " Boston Evening Transcript,
    (19 April 1922), p. 5.
        The novel is "a story of dreary pessimism, " and
    "the harsh and obscure style and the depression of its philoso-
    phy will hardly make this one widely read in America. "

28. "Medaillons--IV: Mr. E. M. Forster, The Spirit of
    Beethoven, " Times (London), (17 June 1922), 14, col. 1.
        The article praises EMF's description of Beethoven's
    C-Minor Symphony as the "only endurable description of that
    symphony. It enables us to understand the inner spirit of all
    his [EMF's] works and may also be why he has left off writing. "

29. "Mr. E. M. Forster's Books, " Times (London), (19

June 1922), 14, col. 2, bottom.
     A letter noting that the writer of "Medaillons" [q. v.
28] failed to mention in his article that EMF is also the author of WAFT and LJ.

30. Sidgwick, F. "Mr. E. M. Forster's Books," Times
     (London), (10 June 1922), 14, col. 5, bottom.
     A letter from the owner of Sidgwick and Jackson,
Ltd. noting an offer to forward a copy of Celest to any
writer of repute who indicates that he has never heard of
EMF. The letter ends with an indication of the correspondent's disbelief that there is any "cultured" individual who
has not heard of EMF.

31. "A Tragic Hero," Springfield Republican, Magazine and
     Feature Section, (29 October 1922), 79.
     A review of LJ. The novel is similar in theme to
Willa Cather's One of Ours, which treats of the same "tragedy of sensibility, imaginativeness and a delicate sense of
honor thwarted by the world." The tone of LJ, however, is
"more conciously literary; the prose richer in shading and
more assured--also more impregnated with Meredithian subtlety."

                              1923

32. "The Celestial Omnibus" (review), Booklist, XX (Nov
     1923), 56.
     The book is a collection of stories in which "fact
and fantasy, the real and the unreal, are delicately blended
and in which the allegory or hidden meaning is sometimes so
veiled as to be bewildering"; nevertheless, they are "marked
by poetic quality."

33. Dickinson, G. Lowes. "Mr. Forster's New Book,"
     Literary Review of the New York Evening Post, (30 June
     1923), 800.
     A review of PP. "The writer of whom he most re-
minds us is Anatole France," but EMF is "humorous instead
of witty." Behind his skepticism "possibly there lurks the
uneradicable English belief that nevertheless the labyrinth has
a key."

34. Forman, Henry James. "Tardy Recognition of an English
     Novelist's Qualities," New York Times, (4 Feb 1923), Sect.
     III, 3 col. 1.
     A review of RWV. "Every novel of EMF ought to

carry in its title the phrase 'with a view.' There is a view
in every one--the most tolerant, penetrating, enlightened view
possible to a novelist." It is "impossible for him to be dull
and stuffy." Though he is a classicist, he is "warm."

35.   "Forster's Alexandria," New York Times Book Review,
      (2 Sept 1923), 15.
         A review of PP. EMF uses an art "so simple as to
seem almost naive." His brief pictures hark back to no
models. The book's success is due to his "finely poised intellect" and his "unforced but leavening humor."

36.   Murry, John Middleton. "The Magic of E. M. Forster,"
      New Republic, XXXV (8 Aug 1923), 293.
         A review of PP. EMF is "at the center of his subject
and the center of himself." Alexandria, "refracted" through
his mind, "becomes a manifestation of himself." There is a
"vortex" in Alexandria into which he was drawn and it resulted
in the "glittering shimmering magic" of the book. EMF is
"behaving oddly and glancing sideways at creation" and "this is
why we remember his former books which were not exactly
good books; sometimes they were almost childish books, but
they were in parts peculiar."

37.   "Pharos and Pharillon" (review), Boston Evening Tran-
      script, (22 Sept 1923), 5.
         The book is a "varied and colorful history of an an-
cient city" and EMF "makes it one of sparkle and delight."

38.   "Short Notices," Spectator, CXXX (30 June 1923), 1089-
      1090.
         A review of PP. "If, as EMF says, the history of
Alexandria is yet to be written, surely he is the man to do it,
even if we must thereby renounce a successor to HE and
RWV."

39.   "Things That Have Interested Mr. Forster," New States-
      man, XXI (16 June 1923), 302.
         A review of PP. It is "regretable that he has not in-
cluded ... chapters to correspond with the admirable sketches"
in the guide-book to Alexandria. The only "admissable com-
plaint is that it contains only eighty pages."

40.   "A Vision of Alexandria," Times Literary Supplement
      (London), (31 May 1923), 369.
         A review of PP. Alexandria, seen through the mind
of EMF, becomes a "manifestation of himself." PP, except

for one essay that "recalls Mr. Lytton Strachey," is "wholly peculiar and wholly good," not like his former books which were "not exactly good books." [This review is probably by John Middleton Murry. see: #36.]

1924

41.   Gaines, Clarence H.   "Some Philosophers in Fiction,"
      North American Review, CCXX (Dec 1924), 375.
            A review of PI. EMF could not have written "so effectively ... about the futility of attempts at social rapprochement between English people and natives of India, if he had not had as the background of his thought the possible futility of all life." Yet "he is anything but depressing." His "wit is unconscionable, but never unkind or atrocious."

42.   Gorman, Herbert S.   "Challenge and Indictment in E. M.
      Forster's Novel: Fresh Evidence that 'East is East and West is West' in A Passage to India," New York Times Book Review, (17 Aug 1924), 6.
            A review of PI. EMF is "undoubtedly one of the finest novelists living in England today." PI is "one of the saddest, keenest, most beautifully written ironic novels of the time," but "one must cultivate a taste for it."

43.   Gould, Gerald.   The English Novel of Today.   London:
      Castle, 1924.   Index.   pp. 152, 183-189.
            "Lovely as his work is, it remains at one remove from life." In HE, EMF asks us "to accept the most blazing impossibilities." This "defect" is also apparent in PI. His medium is not the novel but the "fairy-story." "His weakness is that he cannot lodge his spirits in human bodies."

44.   Gould, Gerald.   "New Fiction," Saturday Review (London),
      CXXXVII (21 June 1924), 642.
            A review of PI. EMF's "medium is really the fairy-story." The one weakness of PI is that he "cannot lodge his spirits in human bodies ... he cannot make them come alive."

45.   Hartley, L. P.   "Mr. Forster's New Novel," Spectator
      (London), CXXXI (28 June 1924), 1048.
            A review of PI. It is the "most considerable" of all novels which have appeared this year. "It surpasses his previous books." It is "intensely personal and ... intensely cosmic." It is a "disturbing, uncomfortable book."

46. "Lovett, Robert Morss. "A Passage to India, " New Re-
     public, XXXX (27 Aug 1924), 393-394.
          A review. EMF has made a "contribution to the
     study of a great historical problem ... as only an artist and
     novelist could make. " He has "developed a novel of manners
     against a background of conquest. " He has "given us a world
     of grotesque and maddening incongruities and absurdities, of
     humor and subtle meaning, of tragic suffering and patient
     striving, and unconquerable sympathy. "

47. "Mr. Forster's India: Subtle and Revealing Picture in
     Notable New Novel, " Springfield Republican, Magazine
     Section, 5A.
          A review of PI. It is impossible to give to those who
     have not read the novel the "faintest notion ... of its total ef-
     fect, because in this case one cannot compare the unknown with
     the known. " EMF "surpasses his former achievements. "

48. Muir, Edwin. "Mr. Forster Looks at India, " Nation,
     CXIX (8 Oct 1924), 379.
          A review of PI. EMF's novel is a work of "inclina-
     tions" adroitly balanced, and "rarely stepping into the faux pas
     of a decision. " PI is a "very comprehensive novel. " His
     theme is "antagonism. " The writing is a "continuous delight. "
     The novel is "a triumph of humanistic spirit over material
     difficult to humanize. "

49. Nevison, Henry W. "India's Coral Strand, " Saturday Re-
     view of Literature (NY), I (16 Aug 1924), 43.
          A review of PI. "The story, though fine and full of
     characters finely suggested, is not the vital or most significant
     part of the work. It is the picture of Anglo-Indian life and
     character on the other hand that is vital and significant. "

50. "New Novels, " Times Literary Supplement (London), (12
     June 1924), 370.
          A review of PI. EMF is exceedingly "fair. " He
     blends "observation and insight" which becomes "his outstand-
     ing virtue. " The novel is as artistic and finished as HE.
     Nevertheless, its form is "stricter" and its appeal "more
     precise. " Its portraiture is "subtle" and has "imaginative
     breadth and generosity. "

51. Miles, E. A. "Oriental Mystery, " Independent, CXIII
     (30 Aug 1924), 134.
          A review of PI. The novel is "a very considerable
     piece of work" which "will not please the Indian Civil Service

... because it takes [a] ... dangerously impractical angle to
the universe."

52. "A Passage to India" (review), <u>Booklist,</u> XXI (Oct 1924),
     27.
        The novel has "subtlety, humor; ... [it is] the mature
work of a thoughtful writer, superbly done."

53. "A Passage to India" (review), <u>Boston Evening Transcript</u>
     (3 Sept 1924), 6.
        PI is a book "worth reading as a story, but ... even
more potent in significance as we realize the subtlety and
power with which EMF has revealed to us the Moslem and
Hindu mind and that ... of the Anglo-Indian."

54. Paterson, Isabel. "Drawing Room Fiction," <u>Bookman</u>,
     LX (24 Dec 1924), 60.
        A review of PI. PI is "probably the best novel of
the year ... the theme is stupendous though the plot is very
simple." The "subtlety of his shading" is "downright uncanny," and "the technique ... is nothing short of wonderful."

55. "Race Conflict in a New Novel," <u>Current Opinion</u>, LXXII
     (Oct 1924).
        A review of PI. EMF's point of view is that of a
"disillusioned observer"; he has "the intellectual detachment
of a John Galsworthy."

56. Redman, Ben Ray. "The Anglo-Indian Problem," <u>Book
     Review</u>, (Sept 1924), 18.
        A review of PI. The novel "is a finished thing ...
written in the firmly restrained but thoroly [sic] capable style
of which EMF proved himself master long ago. Yet ... one
feels that the author has not given fully of his bounty." He
has "utilized the elements of drama, but he has refused to
employ them dramatically. The result is a pictorial rather
than a narrative success."

57. Singh, St. Nihal. "Indians and Anglo-Indians: As Por-
     trayed to Britons by British Novelists," <u>Modern Review</u>,
     XXXVI (Sept 1924), 251-256.
        In PI, EMF's "pictures are faithful and vivid." His
"womenfolk are a vulgar lot." The problem depicted in the
book is essentially "political and not social."

58. Stallings, Laurence. " 'The First Reader': When Rud-
     yards Cease Their Kiplings and Haggards Ride No More,"
     <u>New York World</u>, (13 Aug 1924), 9.

A review of PI. "I doubt that any other book of the fall will supplant A Passage to India as the most sensitive piece of fiction in years." It is "concerned with the transmission of ideas ... between one race and another." Its story is "of the slightest" and a "small hand book of thoughts and 'pensees' could be made from its asides."

59. Watson, Blanche. "A Passage to India" (review), World Tomorrow, VII (Dec 1924), 382.
"Aesthetically the book is good; structurally it is a literary masterpiece; but spiritually it is lacking in insight."

60. Wylie, Elinor. "A Passage to India" (review), New York Tribune, (5 Oct 1924), 1.
EMF "sees so clearly and writes with so magical a fluid, compounded of beauty and ironic salt and limpid clarity, that he is as great a despair to my muddled creative mind as he is an enchantment to my taste and critical faculties."

61. Yust, Walter. "A Passage to India" (review), Literary Review of the New York Evening Post, (16 Aug 1924), 963.
PI is a "careful novel of India.... It is the sort of book which doesn't permit understatement, no matter how wise and protective understatement is."

1926

62. Bullett, Gerald William. Modern English Fiction; A Personal View. London: Jenkins, 1926. pp. 70-85.
In his work, EMF "brings not peace but the sword." He is irresistible if you like him, he is insufferable if you don't, and there is no middle course." The hatred of EMF is due, perhaps, "to his unexpectedness, his elusiveness, his disconcerting possession of qualities which the plainminded like to regard as mutually exclusive."

63. "The English Character," New York Times, (29 Jan 1926), 20, col. 2.
An editorial reaction to EMF's article in The Atlantic Monthly, "Notes on the English Character," January, 1926, vol. 137, pp. 30-37. The writer takes exception to EMF's point of view.

1927

64.   Abbott, Laurence F.   "The Inevitable Leeway," Outlook,
       CXXXXVII (9 Nov 1927),   314.
              A review of Aspects.   EMF's book "is one which will
speed the most constant of readers farther upon the path of his
delight."

65.   "Aspects of the Novel" (review), Saturday Review (London),
       CXLIV (17 Dec 1927),   858.
              "No one is better qualified to write about the novel....
He is our finest living exponent of the novelist's art."

66.   Benson, E. F.   "A Literary Mystification," Spectator
       (London), CXXXIX (29 Oct 1927),   139.
              A review of Aspects.   The volume "is full of ideas
... only just hinted at."   EMF, however, "shows a spark here,
a glimmer there."

67.   Boyd, Ernest.   "Readers and Writers," Independent,
       CXIX (3 Dec 1927),   555.
              A review of Aspects.   EMF is a novelist of "so dis-
tinctive a talent that his views upon the subject of fiction ...
must necessarily command ... attention."   There follows a
summary of the major points discussed in the volume.

68.   "D. H. Lawrence's Novels," Spectator (London), CXXIX
       (6 Aug 1927),   223.
              Before WW I, EMF and D. H. Lawrence seemed the
readers' hopes.   They are "heirs of the great tradition of the
English Novel."   Each "plunged into the dim forest of character
to save himself from chaos."   EMF's world "seemed a
comedy."   He may love a character "like a collector"; he is
"clever and subtle."

69.   Ford, Ford Madox.   "Cambridge on the Caboodle,"
       Saturday Review of Literature (NY), IV (17 Dec 1927),   449.
              A review of Aspects.   EMF's attitude toward the
novel is practically that of "Punch towards the graver problems
of life."   The language in which the book is written is "extremely difficult to understand."

70.   Hutchinson, Percy.   "E. M. Forster Discusses the Art of
       the Novel," New York Times Book Review, (27 Nov 1927),
       2.
              A review of Aspects.   EMF is a "man with an original
turn of mind approaching a fairly threadbare subject in an

original way. There is profit in the book and pleasure." It
"will clarify the mind of any who are given at all to novel-
reading."

71.   "Mr. Forster on the Novel," Times Literary Supplement
      (London), (3 Nov 1927), 784.
          A review of Aspects. The book is a "very thorough
analysis" of the subject. The "wit and vigour make the hap-
piest reading, reinforced as they are by the apparent mischief
of Mr. Forster's businesslike manner."

72.   "New Books in Brief," Independent, CXIX (24 Dec 1927),
      637.
          A review of Aspects. It is no "scholar's handiwork
... no learned treatise, but a series of causeries." While the
book lacks the defects of scholarship, it does not have its
virtues in that it lacks "precision ... definiteness ... [and]
occasionally he sinks to downright vagueness."

73.   Richards, I. A. "A Passage to Forster," Forum,
      (Dec 1927), 914-920.
          There is something "odd" about EMF's method as a
novelist. His oddness has to do with the "special system of
assumptions he tacitly adopts. These assumptions are difficult
to "pin down in words," yet "they influence his handling of
every scene."

74.   Shanks, Edward. "Mr. E. M. Forster," London Mercury,
      XVI (July 1927), 265-274.
          PI was the "final statement for which the others [the
first four novels] were only the drafts, and with it, naturally,
Mr. Forster came to a full stop." But, perhaps, he stopped
because he had "some doubt whether the equipment which had
enabled him to do so much would enable him to do any more."

75.   Woolf, Virginia. "The Art of Fiction," Nation and
      Athenaeum, Lit. Sup., XLII (12 Nov 1927), 247.
          A review of Aspects. EMF's "informal attitude" is
"deliberate" because he is not a scholar. There are, however,
many "judgments that we would willingly argue."

76.   Woolf, Virginia. "Is Fiction an Art?" New York Herald
      Tribune Books, (16 Oct 1927), 1.
          A review of Aspects. Essentially the same as #75.

77.   Woolf, Virginia. "Novels of E. M. Forster," Atlantic
      Monthly, CXL (Nov 1927), 642-648.

EMF is an author about whom there is considerable disagreement. There is something "baffling and evasive in the nature of his gifts." He is extremely susceptible to the influence of time. He has a strong impulse to belong to both camps of novelists, the "preachers and teachers" and "the pure artists." One of the chief problems which confronts him is that of connecting the prose and poetry of life.

1928

78. Beer, T. "The Eternal Moment and Other Stories" (review), New York Evening Post, (12 May 1928), 8.
    The stories are "amusing ... I am not aware of an English writer who can evoke the awkwardness of living more deftly or with so much speed."

79. Connolly, Cyril. "The Eternal Moment" (review), New Statesman, XXX (31 March 1928), 797.
    The stories "though slight ... are all of merit, pagan, supernatural, youthful," but "the central moments ... come out blurred."

80. "The Eternal Moment" (review), Booklist, XXIV (July 1928), 403.
    The volume is a collection of short stories "each embodying a symbolic mood, or changing fantasy touched with delicate irony."

81. "The Eternal Moment" (review), Springfield Republican, (20 May 1928), 7F.
    The reviewer prefers EMF the novelist to EMF the teller of short stories; nevertheless, he finds all of the stories good.

82. "The Eternal Moment" (review), Times Literary Supplement (London), (5 April 1928), 256.
    The "mood rather than the method deserves attention in this collection." The mood is that of "dissatisfaction."

83. Hartley, L. P. "New Fiction," Saturday Review (London), CXLV (28 April 1928), 530.
    EMF is the most "unreviewable of contemporary novelists" because "he succeeds so perfectly in what he sets out to do"; however, the "ironic fantastic tales are the least satisfactory."

84. "Hommage à Monsieur Forster by an Indian, " Nation and
     Athenaeum, XLIII (4 Aug 1928), 589-591.
          There is a danger that PI may be misunderstood by
the majority of Indians because they are used to the "well-
meaning" Englishmen.   EMF is a "sympathizer who has retained his detachment. " He has the "sympathy of an artist. "

85. Kronenberger, Louis.   "E. M. Forster in the Vein of
     Fantasy, " New York Times Book Review, (6 May 1928), 9
          A review of Eternal.   The sixth story ["The Eternal
Moment"] is "unquestionably the finest of them all ... the
other five are altogether worth reading ... they offer us a
new side of Forster. "

86. Muir, Edwin.   "The Eternal Moment" (review), Nation
     and Athenaeum, XXXXIII (12 May 1928), 184.
          "Genius" cannot be denied to certain stories in the
volume.   The best are the "deliberately symbolical, the
stories about Heaven and Hell, and the supernatural in general. "   Of these "The Point of It" and "The Siren's Story" are
perhaps the most remarkable. "

87. "New Novels, " Times (London), (30 March 1928), 22 col.
     5 bottom.
          A review of Eternal.   EMF is "abreast with the
ideas of the modern world. " Fear of the machine and the en-
slavement of man have been expressed before but not with "the
allusive and cutting word" of EMF "nor with his wistful yearning for the finer things once made by man and then lost. "

88. Ross, Mary.   "Forster's Early Tales, " New York Her-
     ald Tribune Book Review, (22 April 1928), 3-4.
          A review of Eternal.   A "rich vein of fantasy. " In
"The Eternal Moment" there is "a clear foreshadowing of
the ... clash of class and race ... in PI. " Collectively the
tales are "fresh and provocative. "

89. Taylor, Rachel Annan.   "The Eternal Moment" (review),
     Spectator, CXXXX (7 April 1928), 543.
          The collection is "distinguished, disillusioned ... with
... cool graces of style.   If it does not captivate it is because
the author is less fortunate with his themes [than he was in
The Celestial Omnibus and Other Stories]"   His "ethic is
definitive and penetrative. "

90. Woolsey, Dorothy Bacon.   "Bards of Passion and of
     Mirth, " New Republic, LVI (29 April 1928), 54.

A review of Eternal. A "collection of lively and
imaginative tales." When D. H. Lawrence [Woolsey also reviews the latter's The Woman Who Rode Away] "lowers in
sultry and oppressive gloom, EMF flashes illuminating fancies
across outlandish vistas." The "deft lightness" of EMF's
"method" in "no way weakens the effect."

1930

91. Mansfield, Katherine. "Throw them Overboard! 'The
     Story of the Siren' by E. M. Forster," in Murry, John
     Middleton, ed. Novels and Novelists. London: Constable
     and Co., 1930. pp. 237-239.
         An analysis of Story. Mansfield finds in it a "certain
leisureliness which is of the very essence of EMF's style"
but "we cannot deny the danger of the writer of drifting ... in
Mr. Forster the danger is particularly urgent because of his
extreme reluctance ... to commit himself."

92. Ward, A. C. The Nineteen-Twenties: Literature and
     Ideas in the Post-War Decade. London: Methuen, 1920.
     Index. pp. 60, 63.
         Virginia Woolf's Voyage Out has an affinity with EMF's
novels; it has the same "sense of life so delicately poised, of
people ... sensitively balanced in thought and feeling." She
shares a limitation, however, with EMF. Their characters
"rarely seem to live" outside their minds.

1931

93. "University News," Times (London), (2 April 1931), 12,
     col. 5.
         At the Spring Graduation ceremony at Aberdeen Uni-
versity, the Honorary Degree of Doctor of Laws (LL.D.) was
conferred upon EMF, among others.

1932

94. Doughty, Howard N., Jr. "Novels of E. M. Forster,"
     Bookman, LXXV (Oct 1932), 542-549.
         Though an important writer, EMF has received "on
the whole very little serious attention from critics of modern
English Literature." One of the reasons for his neglect is the
gap of fourteen years between HE and PI. As a consequence,

PI was reviewed and appreciated without reference to his earlier works and was, therefore, set down as merely a book on India. His work falls "between two worlds." He wrote most of it when Shaw, Bennett and Wells were the mainstream of English literature. He shared little of the "éclat" of his age. Hence he was greeted with "obloquy" when he appeared. His novels do not "come off" as a whole. There is a lack of "integration" in his work. Nevertheless, he is "more clear headed" than D. H. Lawrence. He has demonstrated that it is impossible to restore the individual along the "classic lines of anarchic individualism."

95.   Hutchinson, Percy. "E. M. Forster on Lowes Dickinson," New York Times Book Review, (14 May 1932), 6.
        A review of GLD. The subject of the biography is "adequately displayed and illuminated." In addition to its biographical contents, the book is also a "Lowes Dickinson anthology."

96.   Lawrence, David Herbert. Letters, edited by Aldous Huxley. New York: The Viking Press, 1932. Index. pp. 623, 736; Letters to EMF 228, 558, 621.
        PI "interested" Lawrence "very much" despite the fact that to EMF "India is ... just negative." Lawrence wants "anything [EMF] publishes." He notes that he has seen Murry's "Bou-oum" criticism.

97.   Leavis, Queenie Dorothy. Fiction and the Reading Public. London: Chatto and Windus, 1932. Index. pp. 38, 62, 76-77, 232, 264-265.
        EMF "exposes the inner life" with "illuminating subtlety." There are, in addition, several passing references to EMF.

98.   Ulrich, Kurt. Who Wrote About Whom: A Bibliography of Books on Contemporary British Authors. Berlin: Artur Collingnon, 1932.
        Items #77, 96, 142, 270, 319, 321, 470, 515.

1933

99.   Charques, R. D. Contemporary Literature and Social Revolution. London: Martin Secker, 1933. Index. pp. 90, 122-124, 159.
        EMF's novels "pitchfork us back into the world that still awaited the war it was making." HE "had nothing of the portentious air of closing a period of the English novel.

But that, perhaps, is what it did." PI is a "luminous book,
sensible and ironical and eloquent."

100. Mackenzie, Compton. Literature in My Time. London:
      Rich and Cowan, 1933. Index. pp. 189, 191.
          HE revealed "a new sort of mind" that "while un-
mistakably masculine, was at the same time curiously feminine." Mackenzie's admiration for EMF as a writer is
"unbounded; but a temperamental apathy to his view of life
prevents the least enjoyment of him."

1934

101. Belgion, Montgomery. "The Diabolism of Mr. E. M.
      Forster." Criterion, XIV (Oct 1934), 54-73.
          There is a "mystery" in EMF's work and it is "just
what he stands for." Nevertheless, he is obviously a writer
who has something to say. But "even among his own friends
some have not been altogether certain of the nature of whatever it may be he so obviously tries to bring off." If the
"contrast of the everyday world with the world of values" is
what he stands for, Belgion suspects that many of his values
are "the wrong ones." His "constant mockery" leaves a
"smell of brimstone behind it" because there is no "love" for
humanity in that mockery.

102. Brickell, Herschel. "The Literary Landscape: Por-
      trait of a Humanist," North American Review, CCXXXVIII,
      (Aug 1934), 190.
          A review of GLD. The book "is filled with sympathy
and understanding, in addition to being an admirable piece of
writing."

103. Brown, Edward Killoran. "E. M. Forster and the
      Contemplative Novel," University of Toronto Quarterly,
      III (April 1934), 349-361.
          EMF is the "greatest master of the contemplative
novel in our time." All of his novels are illustrations of a
single idea, "the chasm between the world of action and the
world of being." The typical situation in his work is that of
the "dweller in the world of being who tries to conduct himself in the world of actions according to his inner light, the
light of contemplation."

104. Burra, Peter. "The Novels of E. M. Forster,"
      Nineteenth Century and After, CXVI (Nov 1934), 581-594.

Reprinted as the introduction to Passage to India. London: Dent, Everyman's Library, 1934; and in Malcolm Bradbury, editor. Forster: A Collection of Critical Essays (Twentieth Century Views). Englewood Cliffs, N. J.: Prentice Hall, 1966.

EMF is an "artist on the fringe of social reform"; interested in causes, he has never cut himself off from political and economic questions. He has never deliberately written a novel with a purpose. His novels tell stories that are "monstrous" improbabilities. Nothing of the stories in the first four novels can be believed, but in relation to themselves the books are, nevertheless, beautiful. EMF has developed the art of "clues and chains" to an unusual extent. PI is one of the most aesthetically compact books ever written. Its meaning cannot be defined. EMF is a "musician" who chose the novel because he had ideas to utter. He is passionately interested in humans. HE is an extremely complicated book which can be described as the clash between the business life and the cultured life. He introduces into each of his books an "elemental character." These are Gino (WAFT), Stephen (LJ), George and Mr. Emerson (RWV), Mrs. Wilcox (HE) and Mrs. Moore (PI). EMF has a "faultless sense of style," dazzling humor, and "anonymous prophecy."

105. Dobrée, Bonamy. Modern Prose Style. Oxford: Clarendon Press, 1934. Index. pp. 35-38.
       A stylistic analysis of an unsourced passage from HE.

106. Garnett, David. "Current Literature," New Statesman and Nation, N. S. VII (21 April 1934), 600.
       A review of GLD. An "absolutely delightful" book, but it "leaves out too much." Nevertheless, EMF has created a "living portrait." The "unique merit of this book depends on what there was in common between subject and biographer, particularly ... their sense of humor."

107. "Goldsworthy Lowes Dickinson" (review), Booklist, XXX (July 1934), 348.
       An account of the life and intellectual and emotional development of the late author of A Greek Way of Life, etc., by the author of that "distinguished book" PI.

108. "Goldsworthy Lowes Dickinson" (review), Boston Evening Transcript, (16 June 1934), 1.
       It is "one of the most notable contributions to the history of recent civilization and movements for social and

international reform. "

109. "Goldsworthy Lowes Dickinson" (review), Foreign Af-
      fairs, XIII (Oct 1934), 175.
            The biography is "sympathetic though not uncritical.

109A. "Goldsworthy Lowes Dickinson" (review), Times
      (London), (24 April 1934), 192.
            The detachment in the book is the result "not of even
the slightest absence of sympathy on the smallest point" but
rather of the detachment of "the artist. " EMF is "acutely
conscious that the biographer cannot give so complete a picture of his subject as the novelist of his characters. "

110. Lovett, Robert Morss. "Portrait of a Gentleman, "
      New Republic, LXXX (26 September 1934), 192.
            A review of GLD. EMF possesses "unusual qualifi-
cations for his task. He is a novelist of peculiar gift in
scenting the rare, strange, elusive traits of personality. "

110A. "Lowes Dickinson, " Times Literary Supplement
      (London), (19 April 1934), 279.
            A review of GLD. The chief merit of the book is
its "research. " He has traced with "admirable diligence the
long and complicated story of his friend's intellectual and
emotional development. "

111. Peel, Robert. "Latter-Day Platonist, " Christian Sci-
      ence Monitor, (9 June 1934), 14.
            A review of GLD. To follow GLD "down the years
under the companionable guidance of Mr. E. M. Forster is
for the discriminating an EVENT. " There is a "curious in-
formality of the procedure. "

112. "Philosopher Prophet, " Saturday Review (London),
      CLVIII (8 Sept 1934), 88.
            A review of GLD. The biography is so "solid" that
we get few glimpses into the mind of GLD. EMF does not
gloss over the weaknesses of GLD. As biography, the work
is "monumental. "

113. Sheppard, J. T. "Lowes Dickinson, " Spectator (London),
      CLII (27 April 1934), 664.
            A review of GLD. "A portrait simply and beautifully
done" but also it is the story of a "spiritual quest and an
heroic life of service. "

114. Singh, Bhupal. A Survey of Anglo-Indian Fiction.
     London: Oxford University Press, 1934. Index. pp.
     221-232, 233.
         PI is an "oasis in the desert of Anglo-Indian fiction."
It is "refreshing in its candour, sincerity, fairness, and
art." It is a fascinating study of the problems arising out of
the contact of India with the West." Yet, "it aims at no solution, and offers no explanation" to problems.

115. Swinnerton, Frank Arthur. Georgian Scene. New York:
     Farrar and Rinehart, 1934. Index. pp. 52, 298, 344,
     347, 374, 384, 390-401, 409, 487.
         EMF's books are "luminous demonstrations of cause
and effect." They hold "little warmth," but are, nevertheless, "full of fluctuating imaginative conceptions."

116. Tigner, Hugh Stevenson. "An Urbane Critic of Society,"
     Christian Century, LI (12 Sept 1934), 1150.
         A review of GLD. EMF "has been unable to give us
[the] drama [of GLD'S] spiritual adventure." So far as
biography is concerned, the book runs like the report of an
"urbane certified accountant."

117. Trilling, Lionel. "Politics and the Liberal," Nation
     (NY), CXXXIX (4 July 1934), 24.
         A review of GLD. EMF has "so understandingly
portrayed [the] attitude and the temper of the middle-class
mind that embraces it because they are largely his own."

118. "Two Literary Lives" (review of GLD and Edith
     Wharton's Backward Glance), Current History, XL (Sept
     1934), vii-xii.
         GLD and Edith Wharton are akin in more respects
than one. EMF's biography of GLD is a "candid appraisal,
written with restraint and amazing deftness, and might well
serve as a model for future literary executors."

119. Van Doren, Carl. "A Gentler Socrates in a Safer
     Athens: Forster the Novelist Writes a Delicate Biography
     of Lowes Dickinson's Sensitive Mind," New York Herald
     Tribune Books, (10 June 1934), 5.
         A review of GLD. EMF raises a "monument to a
mind" and the book "is frankest about that part of Dickinson
which claimed no privacy for itself." It is filled with "insight
and grace."

120. Wells, Herbert George. Experiment in Autobiography.
      New York: Macmillan, 1934. Index. p. 593.
          Wells notes that EMF, in his life of GLD, ascribes
the invention of the name "League of Nations" to Aneurin
Williams.

121. Wingfield-Stratford, Esme. "The Last Victorian,"
      Saturday Review of Literature (NY), X (9 June 1934), 739.
          A review of GLD. The reviewer feels the work ad-
mirable but prefers his own memories of GLD to those of
EMF.

                             1935

122. "Goldsworthy Lowes Dickinson" (review by Mc M),
      Catholic World, CXL (Feb 1935), 630-631.
          The biography conveys the charm of its subject while
giving the reader the "peculiar literary thrill of seeing a theme
and its expression as closely suited as hand to glove." It has
a "lucid and plastic style."

                             1936

123. "Abinger Harvest" (review), Booklist, XXXII (July 1936),
      314-315.
          The volume consists of "scattered writings collected
from periodicals of the last thirty years."

124. "Abinger Harvest" (review), Wisconsin Library Bulletin,
      XXXII (Oct 1936), 98.
          A "miscellany of writing, part of which are a group
of critical essays including one on Sinclair Lewis which will
probably be of greatest interest to American readers."

125. "Books in Brief," Christian Century, LIII (15 July 1936),
      991.
          A review of AH. EMF is "equally gifted as novelist
essayist, and critic." His essays are "keen, provocative, en-
tertaining, learned--and whatever else good essays should
be."

126. "Books of the Week: Mr. E. M. Forster's Essays, A
      Varied Harvest," Times (London), (20 March 1936), 19,
      col. 1.
          A review of AH. EMF has as many ideas and as

fertile as any contemporary writer of fiction. More, indeed,
than he has ever managed to make use of as a novelist. This
volume is a "luxury of his mind."

127. Bowen, Elizabeth. "Abinger Harvest" (review),
     Spectator (London), CLVI (20 March 1936), 521.
          The order of the essays is "vital." One should fol-
low the order in reading them. The dates, however, play no
part in the arrangement of the essays and ought not. "There
never seems to have been an early work ... his maturity is
innate." To criticism, EMF brings "the makeup of the artist."
His prose is "the prose of the novels."

128. Brickell, Herschel. "The Literary Landscape: A Num-
     ber of Things," Review of Reviews XCIV (July 1936),
     12-13.
          A review of AH. The book is "filled with excellent
writing and clear thinking" and is "worthy of study by everyone who likes the best English prose and a genuinely liberal
point of view."

129. Dangerfield, George. "Scenario of a Civilized Mind,"
     Saturday Review of Literature (NY), XIV (30 May 1930), 7.
          A review of AH. EMF is a master of English prose.
AH proves it. It is a pity, however, that the book is a collection of essays and not a novel. Anyone who misses reading
it, nevertheless, will be "missing one of the most exquisite
pleasures that the contemporary market can afford."

130. Garnett, David. "Current Literature," New Statesman
     and Nation (London), NS. XI (21 March 1936), 459.
          A review of AH. "EMF has brought the most well-
timed precious comfort in AH." It is a "feast of scraps offered when the cook is too lazy to provide a fresh roast. Yet
these scraps define EMF more exactly than any of the novels."
The book is one of the "most delightful collections of occasional writings I have read."

131. Henderson, Philip. The Novel Today: Studies in Con-
     temporary Attitudes. London: Lane, 1936. Index. pp.
     19, 20-23, 28, 43, 91-96, 248, 251.
          PI is a "courageous and admirable book." Unfor-
tunately, EMF "fails to see his unbearable British officials as
the instruments of a deliberately planned colonial policy." PI
"does not go far enough in its criticism of conditions in India."

132. Jack, Peter Monro. "E. M. Forster's Delightful

Essays, " New York Times Book Review, (24 May 1936),
2.
       A review of AH. EMF is "all order and coherence."
However, "The Present" is "appallingly limited." The piece
on Mickey Mouse is "desultory." The essays devoted to
books are "so much better." EMF "speaks for the older
generation and writes to the new."

133. Jones, E. B. C. "E. M. Forster and Virginia Woolf"
      in Derek Verschoyle, ed. The English Novelists: A Sur-
      vey of the Novel by Twenty Contemporary Novelists.
      New York: Harcourt Brace and Co., 1936. pp. 281-300.
       In EMF's works "the method of the mid-nineteenth
century novelist is in full swing." While "fluent" over
mental crises, he is "terse" over the physical. Besides
sentimentality, there is one other resemblance to be noted
between Virginia Woolf and EMF: "that of half-heartedness
about sexual love."

134. Kelly, Blanche Mary. The Well of English. New York:
      Harper and Bros., 1936. Index. p. 320.
       EMF's work represents an "attitude of nonchalance in
love, what Lawrence called the 'insouciance which is so lovely
in free animals and plants.'" HE is an "astounding anticipation of the post-war [WWI] novel."

135. Kronenberger, Louis. "Mr. Forster's Harvest,"
      Nation, CXLII (17 June 1936), 780-781.
       A review of AH. EMF, "though neither a writer of
the first rank nor a writer who satisfies our most pressing
needs ... is one with a peculiar value and charm." AH is
"not a bad index to his character and talents." It is "a
harvest of scattered and sometimes dated grain [with] no
sense of art in it."

136. Littell, Philip. "E. M. Forster," New Republic,
      LXXXVII (8 July 1936), 273.
       A review of AH. EMF is a "good guide to past
times and distant presents." The beauty of the book is "omni-
present." No contemporary mind as penetrating and generaliz-
ing as EMF's "lives so close to sense data. What he thinks of
is of less interest to him and to us than what he perceives."

137. "Mr. E. M. Forster Past and Present," Times Liter-
      ary Supplement (London), (21 March 1936), 239.
       A review of AH. The volume is a "rich and diverse"
collection. "Imaginative realism which sees and accepts life,

naked and whole" is the great characteristic of these essays as
it is of his five novels.

138.   Patterson, Isabel.   "Mr. Forster, Cultured, Tolerant,
         Urbane, " New York Herald Tribune Books, (31 May 1936),
         6.
              A review of AH.   "The whole book offers a very
worth-while acquaintance with a cultured, tolerant and urbane
mind. "   Though it does contain some pieces which are
"strangely faded. "

139.   Pritchett, V. S.   "Abinger Harvest" (review), Chris-
         tian Science Monitor, (29 April 1936), 11.
              EMF's writing is marked by "integrity and good
sense. "   He has a wily and wiry vigor. "

140.   Ransom, John Crowe.   "Gestures of Dissent, " Yale
         Review, NS. XXVI (Aut 1936), 181.
              A review of AH.   ". . . one of the notable literary
miscellanies of our time. "

141.   Reilly, Joseph J.   "Made by Time. " Commonweal,
         XXV (25 Dec 1936), 251+.
              A review of AH.   As a critic, EMF is uneven.   His
study of Proust is "unsatisfying, " that of T. S. Eliot, "inadequate, " but the essay on Sinclair Lewis is "keen. "   EMF is
at his best when picturing men.   The volume is "interesting,
[and] worthwhile. "   It is by an author who is "sane, sensitive
and [a] delightful writer. "

142.   Schell, Jonathan.   "Books: A Causerie, " Forum,
         XCVI (July 1936), iv.
              A review of AH.   The volume is "a great pleasure
to read. "   It is filled with "rich enlightenment, humor, and
knowledge. "

143.   Sélincourt, Basil de.   "Abinger Harvest" (review),
         Manchester Guardian (20 March 1936), 7.
              The book has "wide and gracious sympathies ...
delicacy of style [and] occasional illumination. "

144.   Simonds, Katherine.   "Sketches by a Novelist, "
         Atlantic Monthly, CLVIII (Aug 1936), no p. #, under
         "The Atlantic Bookshelf. "
              A review of AH.   EMF's "analysis has ever the
color of fiction. "

145. Swinnerton, Frank Arthur. "Abinger Harvest" (review),
      Chicago Daily Tribune, (14 March 1936), 14.
          The collection is as "enjoyable as many novels." It
is "full of lucidity."

146. Swinnerton, Frank Arthur. Swinnerton: An Auto-
      biography. Hutchinson, 1936.

                              1937

147. "Cold Water on a Show," New York Times, (8 April
      1937), 22, col. 3.
          An editorial. The writer offers a negative reaction
to EMF's article in the Spectator (London), "Coronation Night-
mare." He notes that "if millions ... are eager to see the
show, why should EMF grudge them their pleasure?" Perhaps, he recommends, "skittles and beer would rid Mr.
Forster of his doleful dumps."

148. "Law Report, Feb. 18," Times (London), (19 Feb
      1937), 4, col. 2.
          A record of EMF's involvement in a libel action
brought by Sir Murdoch Macdonald against him and Arnold,
his publisher, claiming that EMF had libeled him in AH.

149. Lawrence, A. W. T. E. Lawrence by His Friends.
      London: Jonathan Cape, 1937.
          Speaks of the EMF - T. E. Lawrence friendship.

150. "Literary Awards," Times (London), (18 Feb 1937),
      11, col. 4.
          A note to the effect that EMF was presented with the
A. C. Benson Silver Medal of the Royal Society of Literature
in recognition of his service to literature.

151. Routh, Harold Victor. Toward the Twentieth Century.
      Cambridge (Eng): Cambridge University Press, 1937.
      Index. pp. 161, 181, 385.
          EMF was influenced by the "inductions of Bergson."
EMF was among the last "to echo Matthew Arnold's quest of
spiritual self-possession and the welter of intellectual dis-
tractions."

152. Traversi, D. A. "The Novels of E. M. Forster,"
      Arena I (April 1937), 28-40.
          EMF's work springs from "a critical balance, from

a continual concern for the wholeness and harmony of life. "
The acceptance of Auden and Eliot of their respective dogmas
is "an attempt to shelter themselves from their own poverty
of life. " How far EMF "succeeds in criticizing this poverty,
and how far he transcends it by his own qualities, are the pro-
posed aims of this essay. "

153.   Warren, Austin. "Novels of E. M. Forster, " Ameri-
       can Review, IX (Summer 1937), 226-251.
           EMF expounded, in Aspects, the Jamesian theory of
the novel only to reject or minimize it.   He believes it
dangerous for the author to take the reader into his confi-
dence about his characters, but not dangerous about the universe.   In theory and practice, EMF allows the novelist
latitude.   The novel has its function: that of the "art of
equilibrium. " His England is that of the upper middle classes and the intelligentsia.   His "humanity will know all. " His
first three novels (WAFT, LJ, RWV) keep to "the sunlight of
realism. " WAFT and RWV are "high comedy. " In HE,
EMF introduces the "double vision"; in PI, Celest, and Eternal there is an "hysterical element. "

                              1938

154.   Dangerfield, George. "E. M. Forster: A Man With a
       View, " Saturday Review of Literature (NY), XVIII (27
       Aug 1938), 3-4, 14-16.
           EMF is in many ways a "disconcerting writer. " He
has produced little; nevertheless, he is a "major novelist. "
It is often difficult to discover "what he is driving at. " In
him can be discovered the "mysterious operations of the
liberal temperament. "

155.   Dobree, Bonamy. Introductions to English Literature.
       Vol. IV. London: The Cresset Press, 1938. pp. 100-101.
           EMF's novels are the "deepest reaction" against the
things Kipling stood for.   Both writers, however, are typical
of the Edwardian period.   For EMF, the important things are
"the inner things. " His prose is "delicate, accurate, pre-
cise. " His characters are "jealous of their integrity. "

156.   Macaulay, Rose. The Writings of E. M. Forster.
       London: Hogarth Press, 1938.
           The volume is more of an appreciation than a critical
study.   WAFT belongs to "a young and emotional world. " She
finds LJ "the most personal and the most universal of the

five novels; and obviously the most autobiographical." RWV
is "clearer and brighter, and possibly better constructed ...
and thinner in the sense of being less full and rich. But it
has a wit, a gay brilliance, that belongs, perhaps, to EMF's
notion of Italy." HE is a "rich work of delicate social
irony." In PI "there is greater seriousness and depth, even
sadness, more poetry, more beauty, less wit" than in his
earlier works. The volume is liberally sprinkled with biographical information as well as insights into the writing of
his books.

157. Zabel, Morton Dauwen. "E. M. Forster," Nation,
      CXLVII (22 Oct 1938), 412-413+.
          EMF offers few appeals which today qualify for
popularity. There are no dogmatic beliefs in politics or social thought, no stylistic novelty, no yearly appeals to his
public with a new book. Yet, the attraction he has as a
novelist has been strong even from his first novel.

                            1939

158. Connolly, Cyril. Enemies of Promise. Boston: Little
      Brown, 1939. Index. pp. 7, 31-32, 62, 107, 122, 158.
          Much of EMF's art "consists in the plainness of his
writing." HE shows a "great departure from the writing of
the nineteenth century." He displays "extreme simplicity,
the absence of relative and conjunctive clauses, and everyday
choice of words." LJ and HE established a "point of view, a
technique, and an attitude ... that were to be followed by
psychological novelists for another thirty years."

159. Garnett, David, ed. The Letters of T. E. Lawrence.
      New York: Doubleday, 1939. Index.
          PI is "more like sculpture" than a novel because it
is a "three or four-sided thing." It is "extraordinarily satisfying." EMF can "shape so spare and trim a thing out of an
innumerable heap of impressions." He is a "great writer,"
and a "subtle and helpful critic." There are additional
critical remarks on Aspects, Celest, GLD, HE, LJ, PI, PP,
and Story.

                            1940

160. Datalier, Roger [pseud. of A. A. Eaglestone]. The
      Plain Man and the Novel. London: Nelson, 1940. Index.

pp. 165-169.
     In PI, EMF "poses the issue by bringing together two highly intelligent men, one Fielding, an Englishman ... and the other, Dr. Aziz, a Hindu medico." The book is "a satire of contrasts through which perhaps the irreconcilable may be reconciled by such an attitude as that displayed by Fielding and Mrs. Moore."

161. Reid, Forrest. <u>Private Road</u>. London: Faber and Faber, 1940, pp. 58, 77, 85, 115-116, 239-241.
     Reid disputes EMF's remark in AH that Ronald Firbank "had genius." Reid notes that EMF felt that his, Reid's, publisher was correct in extending <u>The Bracknels</u>. He recounts his first meeting with EMF (pp. 115-116).

1942

162. Adams, J. Donald. "Speaking of Books," <u>New York Times Book Review</u>, (26 July 1942), 2.
     Adams takes exception to EMF's remark that he does not think that there will be any more professional writers.

163. "Along the Bookshelves," <u>Churchman</u>, CLVI (1 Dec 1942), 17.
     A review of VW. The reviewer finds EMF's essay "enthusiastic."

164. Burnham, David. "The Invalid Lady of Bloomsbury," <u>Commonweal</u>, XXXVI (2 Oct 1942), 567-568.
     A review of VW and David Daiches' <u>Virginia Woolf</u>. The reviewer notes that EMF believed Virginia Woolf "not a great creator of character."

165. Colum, Mary M. "Heir to Tradition and Free to Experiment," <u>New York Herald Tribune Books</u>, (4 Oct 1942), 34.
     A review of VW and Virginia Woolf's <u>The Death of the Moth</u>. "Not since Paul Valery's address to the French Academy on the work of his predecessor in the fortieth chair, Anatole France, have we had such an ingenious, though in this case, perhaps, unconscious, denigration of a dead author by a living one." EMF's work shows "little appreciation." He claims that Virginia Woolf was "over esthetic and barely escaped being 'arty'."

166. "A Crown of Laurel: Virginia Woolf by E. M. Forster,"

Spectator (London), CLXVIII (5 June 1942), 540.
A review of VW. EMF "attempts not judgement but
justification." He presents not the "invalid lady of Bloomsbury" but "a civilized being" for he "sees her limitations and
her virtues."

167.   "The Death of the Moth by Virginia Woolf," New Yorker,
       XVIII (26 Sept 1942), 80.
A note that one of the best essays in the collection is
that on EMF.

168.   Dunbar, Olivia Howard.   "Virginia Woolf: A Review of
       Virginia Woolf's Death of the Moth; E. M. Forster's Vir-
       ginia Woolf; David Daiches' Virginia Woolf," New Repub-
       lic, CVII (12 Oct 1942), 471-472.
EMF has managed to note, despite the few pages of
his "admirable" essay, "most of the important things about
Mrs. Woolf." He is less concerned with "determining her
rank as a writer" than in "amplifying the existing notion of
her as a human being." The most significant thing that he
says about her is that she had a "singleness of purpose."

169.   Frierson, W. C.   "Years 1900-1915," in The English
       Novel in Transition.   Norman, Oklahoma: University of
       Oklahoma Press, 1942.   Index. pp. 168-72.
In his novels, EMF uses a technique that in part belongs to previous generations. Yet there are few authors
more influenced than he by the ideas of his day. He follows
H. G. Wells in feeling that civilization is "out of joint."
EMF was the "chief influence on D. H. Lawrence." All of his
novels have an intellectual element.

170.   Gregory, Horace.   "Virginia Woolf's 'The Death of the
       Moth': A Posthumous Collection of Essays--and E. M.
       Forster's Tributary Lecture," New York Times Book Re-
       view, (27 Sept 1942), 2, 20.
A review of VW. EMF's remarks are of more "penetrating eloquence" than Virginia Woolf's notations on his novels.
He celebrates "the pervading charm of her personality."
What he says reflects "the sensibility of an inhabitant of Virginia Woolf's world as well as one who traveled beyond its
sphere."

171.   Kronenberger, Louis.   "Virginia Woolf as Critic,"
       Nation, CLV (17 Oct 1942), 382-385.
A review of VW, Virginia Woolf's Death of the Moth,
and David Daiches' Virginia Woolf. EMF's work is "charming

yet candid, full of sharp comments and animating touches, but
too short to say all that it might. "

172. Mortimer, Raymond. "Books in General, " New States-
      man and Nation, NS XXIII (13 June 1942), 390.
            A review of VW. The essay is "a summing up ex-
emplary in its shrewdness and delicacy. "

173. Roberts, R. Ellis. "A Biographer Manquée, " Satur-
      day Review of Literature (NY), XXV (3 Oct 1942), 9.
            A review of VW. EMF "understands biography so
little that he praises Virginia Woolf's Roger Fry. " He calls
her a "snob. "

174. Stonier, G. W. "Books in General, " New Statesman
      and Nation, XXIV (21 Nov 1942), 613.
            A review of the Everyman Edition of PI with an intro-
duction by Peter Burra. EMF won't "let his characters go. "
He is a "half-hog" writer, unlike Virginia Woolf who is
"whole-hog. " The only faults in PI are Mrs. Moore, "who
collapses suddenly and becomes a hateful mummy, " and "the
lukewarm lovers, Ronny and Adela. "

175. Tillotson, Geoffrey. Essays in Criticism and Research.
      Cambridge, Eng.: The University Press, 1942. Index.
      pp. 201-203.
            The "parabolic element, " the "philosophy" in "Mr.
Andrews, " and "Co-ordination" are so pronounced as to find
"almost aphoristic expression. "

176. Trilling, Lionel. "E. M. Forster, " Kenyon Review,
      IV (Spring 1942), 160-173.
            Essentially the same material which is expanded in
his book-length study, q. v. #189.

177. "Virginia Woolf" (review), Times Literary Supplement
      (London), (23 May 1942), 260.
            A "sadly slim, little booklet. " EMF indicates that
Virginia Woolf was "sensitive but tough. " The essay is an
"admirable account of her whole work. "

                              1943

178. Adams, J. Donald. "Speaking of Books, " New York
      Times Book Review, (10 Oct 1943), 2.

"Nobody has put more clearly the vital hold which the novel has ... than EMF, [who is] one of the few novelists who have written illuminatingly about their own craft." The remainder of the article discusses EMF's theories of fiction reflected in Aspects.

179. Adams, J. Donald. "Speaking of Books," New York
      Times Book Review, (31 Oct 1943), 2.
          Adams notes that EMF, as far back as 1929, pre-
dicted that the latter stages of the development of Sinclair
Lewis as a writer were "bound to be disappointing."

180. "Current Revival of Interest in E. M. Forster's
      Novels," Publishers' Weekly, CXLIV (25 Sept 1943),
      1161-1162.
          Publication data is given on the American reprints of
WAFT, HE, LJ, RWV.

181. "First American Publisher," Publishers' Weekly, CXLIV
      (16 Oct 1943), 1518.
          The first American publisher of any of EMF's novels
was Putnam, which published RWV and HE in 1911. By the
time Knopf decided to publish the novels after World War I,
the plates had been melted down and the rights reverted to
EMF.

182. "Forster and the Human Fact," Time, XLII (9 Aug
      1943), 98+.
          A review of E. M. Forster by Lionel Trilling. The
volume, part biography and part criticism, attempts to tell
why there is a recent renewal of interest in EMF. The heart
of the book is the "brilliant" chapter called "Forster and the
Liberal Imagination." It is a "shrewd study" of the liberal
mind and the "first successful attempt to set EMF in the context of his time."

183. Godfrey, Eleanor. "Unbuttoned Manner," Canadian
      Forum, XXIII (Oct 1943), 154-155.
          EMF rebelled against the "self-conscious, power-
ridden, proprietorial society" but "unlike Shaw, he refused to
crusade."

184. Jones, Howard Mumford. "E. M. Forster and the
      Liberal Imagination," Saturday Review of Literature (NY),
      XXVI (28 Aug 1943), 6-7.
          A review of Lionel Trilling's E. M. Forster; and of
RWV, LJ, HE, WAFT, which were republished in 1943.

EMF conveys to us the "serene maturity of an epoch now
patronized only by vulgar and opinionated minds." Trilling
says many "shrewd things about EMF's central theme." Im-
plicit, also, in his discussion is "the splendor and strength
of the liberal tradition." This gives "body and insight into
EMF's novels."

185. Mayberry, George. "The Forster Revival," New Re-
     public, CIX (6 Sept 1943), 341.
          Mayberry notes the reprinting of WAFT, LJ, RWV,
HE and the publication of Lionel Trilling's E. M. Forster.
The latter, he indicates, is an "excellent introduction to EMF
and his works. Trilling focuses upon EMF as a "deliberate
artist," unlike the "rambling appreciation" by Rose Macaulay
[q.v. #156].

186. Pryce-Jones, Alan. "Books in General," New States-
     man and Nation, NS XXVI (6 Nov 1943), 303.
          A review of Lionel Trilling's E. M. Forster.
Trilling's volume is "a concise, critical guidebook." Because he writes from Columbia University, however, he "misses some of EMF's finer points." Nevertheless, he "adequate-
ly" exhibits the "bones," but "subtleties of nerve and com-
plexion" are sometimes missing.

187. Ransom, John Crowe. "Editorial Notes: E. M.
     Forster," Kenyon Review, V (Autumn 1943), 618-623.
          "... five separate times [EMF] has taken a set of
characters, indisputably alive ... and studied them ... with
uncanny and merciless intelligence. They are we." His
novels are "explosive."

188. Schorer, Mark. "Virginia Woolf," Yale Review, NS
     XXXII (winter 1943), 377-381.
          A review of EMF's VW and Virginia Woolf's The
Death of the Moth. Schorer notes that EMF maintained that
Virginia Woolf's characters "never seem unreal; ... [but] one
does not remember them." Schorer cannot accept this judgment.

189. Trilling, Lionel. E. M. Forster. Norfolk, Connecticut:
     New Directions, 1943; London: Hogarth Press, 1944.
          Without a doubt, one of the landmarks of Forster-
criticism. The tone of the volume and, unhappily, much of
what has been written about EMF since its publication, is set
in its introduction: "Forster and the Liberal Imagination."
Frederick P. W. McDowell, in his E. M. Forster, notes

that the volume is "valuable more for esthetic than for political
and philosophical judgments; Trilling's doctrinaire liberalism
obtrudes too greatly."   Chapter II: Sawston and Cambridge
offer biographical information.   Trilling sets aside a chapter
for each of the novels and one for the short stories, exploring
their themes.   His final chapter discusses EMF's literary
criticism.   A bibliography of EMF's major works is followed
by a brief listing of works "on Forster."

190. Wright, Cuthbert.   "Damned and the Saved," Common-
        weal, XXXVIII (24 Sept 1943), 557-561.
                There is a "barricade" running through EMF's novels
with "mighty opposites of Good and Evil arrayed on one side
and the other."   With him, these forces are apt to take the
form of "fertility" and "sterility," and "unawareness" and "integration; life and death."   The protagonists of these forces
sometimes change sides in the middle and often in "the most
remarkable manner."

191. Zabel, Morton Dauwen.   "Forster Revival," Nation,
        CLVII (7 Aug 1943), 158-159.
                A review of Lionel Trilling's E. M. Forster.   The
volume is the "best" full study of EMF's works and ideas
yet written.   It takes on the force of "a public service."

                                    1944

192. Annan, Noel.   "Books in General," New Statesman
        and Nation, NS XXVIII (7 Oct 1944), 239-240.
                A review of Lionel Trilling's E. M. Forster.
Though Trilling is a scholar, it is upon a point of scholarship that his "thesis is perhaps thrown very slightly out of
true alignment."

193. "A Birthday and a Moral: The National Gallery Con-
        certs," Times (London), (13 Oct 1944), 6.
                A news item to the effect that last Tuesday [7 Oct
1944] the National Gallery published a book in honor of the
fifth anniversary of its concerts.   In it is recorded all the
music performed at more than 1300 concerts including tributes from individuals in other arts.   One of these tributes is
from EMF.

194. Brown, E[dward] K[illoran].   "Revival of E. M. Forster,"
        Yale Review, NS XXXIII (June 1944), 668-681.
                For years, EMF has been "scarcely a name to the

general reader" but within 1943 came reprints of RWV, LF,
WAFT, HE. PI was in print in the Modern Library. An
"excellent and sympathetic estimate" of his work was produced by Lionel Trilling, while from "some critics of the extreme left there was faint praise. " EMF in our time has been,
perhaps, the writer who has written the "subtlest ... novel of
ideas in England. " The present revival "will doubtless fail
to make" EMF "a major figure in fiction comparable with
Conrad. "

195. McLuhan, H[erbert] M[arshall]. "Kipling and Forster, "
      Sewanee Review, LII (July-Sept 1944), 332-343.
         EMF's passion for the "melodrama of coincidence"
surpasses Kipling's but is "not different in kind. " It is the
"byproduct of cultural neurosis. " The "hypnotized acceptance
of rigid distinctions is necessary to any kind of violent clash
between characters in such a world. " EMF, like Kipling,
can "only go through the motions of testing ... because everything has really been decided in advance. "

196. Nicholson, Norman. Man and Literature. London:
      S. C. M. Press, 1944. Index. pp. 157-160.
         EMF "subtly debunked" the fantasy of Natural Man
in popular fiction. Of all modern satirists, he is "supreme. "
WAFT's plot is "outrageous. " HE contains "wise and penetrating comment on the relations between people of different
social classes, " and PI is the same on Anglo-Indian problems.
LJ applies more directly to the "myth of Natural Man. "

197. "Tercentenary Celebration in London, " Times (London),
      (23 Aug 1944), 7.
         A news story to the effect that EMF presided at a
five-day conference held by the London Centre of P. E. N. to
commemorate the tercentenary of the publication of Milton's
Areopagitica. In his remarks, EMF noted that, after the war
ends or "eases off, " P. E. N. should insist on less secrecy in
public affairs.

                              1945

198. Adams, J. Donald. "Speaking of Books, " New York
      Times Book Review, (11 Nov 1945), 2.
         "There is no more interesting book on the art of
fiction than EMF's Aspects of Fiction. " The remainder of the
article is devoted to summarizing the major points of
Aspects.

199. Lunan, N. M. "The Novels of E. M. Forster,"
     Durham University Journal, NS VI (March 1945), 52-57.

200. Morton, Arthur Leslie. "E. M. Forster and the Class-
     less Society," in Language of Men. London: Cobbett
     Press, 1945, 78-88.
          EMF writes for an audience "that does not now exist,
     but ... for one that will come into being even though it may
     have waited for a hundred years." He writes for "the class-
     less society that will grow up on the far side of the Revolu-
     tion."

201. Waggoner, Hyatt Howe. "Exercises in Perspective:
     Notes on the uses of Coincidence in the Novels of E. M.
     Forster," Chimera, III (Summer 1945), 3-14.
          EMF's novels suggest "an essentially religious view
     of life." Nevertheless, his fiction never "sums up any
     philosophy." His "mystical naturalism" emerges only as a
     "totality of meaning." He does not attempt to present "life as
     it is." He "enlarges" our vision by "interrupting his action
     with analytical asides." This is his general method. There
     is, however, another way in which he accomplishes this "en-
     largement." This other method has "received too little pene-
     trating comment." EMF uses the device of coincidence ef-
     fectively, even though a number of his critics consider this
     the weakest aspect of his work.

202. Weber, Conrad G. Studies in the English Outlook in the
     Period Between the World Wars. Bern, Switzerland: A.
     Francke, 1945. Index. pp. 47, 163.
          EMF wrote Aspects "not for the sake of analysis but
     to show that the novel is an artistic achievement."

                              1946

203. Adams, J. Donald. "Speaking of Books," New York
     Times Book Review, (17 Nov 1946), 2.
          A discussion of EMF's concept of fiction, drawn
     chiefly from Aspects.

204. Ault, Peter. "Aspects of E. M. Forster," Dublin
     Review, CCXIX (Oct 1946), 109-134.
          If wisdom is found in EMF's novels, it is because
     his subject matter's boundaries are only those of actual life.
     He is an agnostic of the second generation. His characters
     have rejected Christianity except as a guide for behavior in

certain matters, yet they are "haunted" by a memory of religious hope which "persists like the habit of a drug. "

205. Brower, Reuben A. "Beyond E. M. Forster: Part
     I--The Earth, " Foreground, I (Spring-Summer 1946), 164-
     174.
         There is a point in reading the novels of EMF "at
which a certain and harmonious response becomes difficult. "
As LJ, HE, PI are read "we become increasingly aware of
a beauty which we suspect may indicate confusion rather than
profundity and which may conceal basic contradictions. "

206. Connolly, Cyril. "Art of Being Good: A Note on
     Maugham and Forster, " in Condemned Playground. New
     York: Macmillan, 1946, pp. 250-259.
         Connolly holds that EMF, like the Victorians, "be-
lieves that to write simply it is necessary to be good. " In
everything he writes, EMF is a "moralist. " By defining his
creed, he can be best understood. A "clear definition" is
given by Lionel Trilling in his E. M. Forster.

207. Gilomen, W. "Fantasy and Prophecy in E. M.
     Forster's Works, " English Studies, XXVII (Aug 1946), 97-
     112.
         EMF is "a worshipper of Pan. " All of his novels ex-
press "a strange and mysterious atmosphere, " either "by the
mysterious and supernatural which nature and milieu act upon
men or by the quaintness of certain characters. " Prophecy,
to EMF, has a tendency to have "characters and situations
stand for more than themselves. " In his work there can be
discovered a "common undercurrent" of prophecy.

208. Hamill, Elizabeth. These Modern Writers; An Intro-
     duction for Modern Readers. Melbourne, Australia:
     Georgian House, 1946, pp. 137-144.
         EMF's work is a "link between the liberal thought
of the generation of Shaw, Wells and Chesterton and contemporary socialist thought in English literature. " He recognizes the
"need for the artist to participate in the vulgar political conflicts which are shaping the world. " In this he is in "idametri-
cal opposition to Joyce's claim for supreme artistic detachment. "

209. Holt, Lee Elbert. "E. M. Forster and Samuel Butler, "
     Publications of the Modern Language Association, LXI
     (Sept 1946), 804-819.
         EMF should be placed "second only to Shaw" as a

disciple of Samuel Butler. No attempt, however, is made in
supporting this thesis to "prove a literary 'influence'." The
author limits himself to interpretation.

210. Routh, Harold Victor. English Literature and Ideas in
      the Twentieth Century: An Inquiry into Present Diffi-
      culties and Future Prospects. London: Methuen, 1946.
      Index. pp. 58-62, 69.
            EMF's literary and ideological backgrounds are ex-
plored as well as the progress of his "experiments" in the
novel; his "future reputation" is also assessed.

211. Shahani, Ranjee G. "Some British I Admire," Asiatic
      Review. NS XLII (July 1946), 270-273.
            EMF is a "splendid stylist" and has an "astonishing
power of observation," but lacks the supreme gift of the great
artist--the power to shape masses of material into creative
wholes." He is best as a writer of short stories. In his
novels he must use "a great deal of padding."

                              1947

212. Bailey, J. O. Pilgrims Through Space and Time. New
      York: Argus Books, 1947.

213. Baker, Carlos. "E. M. Forster's Quality of Insight,"
      New York Times Book Review, (13 July 1947), 5.
            A review of Collect. The tales "seem ... to em-
brace a unifying theme," i.e. "the materialistic aspects of
the world are too much with us." EMF's heroes and heroines, though assorted, share the single quality of "insight."

214. "Books--Authors," New York Times, (25 April 1947),
      19, col. 2, last item.
            An announcement to the effect that EMF will speak
at Harvard University's symposium of music criticism to be
held "next Thursday and Friday" [May 1-2, 1947].

215. "Collected Tales," Booklist, XLIV (15 Sept 1947), 35.
            A note to the effect that the volume reprints those
stories printed in Celest and Eternal.

216. "Collected Tales" (review), Library Journal, LXXII
      (July 1947), 1033.
            EMF's tales are "less successful than his novels,
but ... important expressions by a major literary figure."

Further, "they show respectability and convention confronted by the pagan virtues."

217. "Collected Tales," New Yorker, XXIII (12 July 1947), 67.
    A note to the effect that EMF's stories have been long out of print in the United States.

218. Downes, Olin. "Composer and Critic: Contrasting Views of Their Relationship Developed at Harvard Symposium," New York Times, (18 May 1947), 7, col. 1.
    A report on the Harvard Symposium in which EMF took part with his talk, "The Raison d'Etre of Criticism in the Arts." Downes found the talk "finished" and "charming," but presenting a point of view which seems to be "contradicted by implicit characteristics" of EMF's works.

219. "Fables in Fantasy," Time, L (11 Aug 1947), 101.
    A review of Collect. No one of EMF's stories "bears the scars of age; their disembodied timelessness is witness to Forster's skill." In them, he "contrasts the simple instincts of people with the taboos and sophistries of social custom."

220. "Fantasy Then and Now," New York Herald Tribune Book Review, (27 July 1947), 14.
    A review of Collect. EMF's stories "deserve to be better known" for they "are delicately conceived and intelligently executed."

221. "Fantasy Without Apology," Christian Science Monitor, (4 Aug 1947), 14.
    A review of Collect. EMF's fantasy "consists in recapturing a sense of the ancient myths underlying the Italian or English woods and valleys." He has the power to "evoke atmosphere" and has a "delicacy of imagination and precision of style."

222. Jackson, J. H. "Collected Tales" (review), San Francisco Chronicle, (25 July 1947), 12.
    EMF's stories are written "with the sureness that has always characterized [his] work and flavored with the delicate irony that is always [his] mark."

223. Liddell, Robert. A Treatise on the Novel. London: Cape, 1947. Index. pp. 44, 56, 64-70, 154, 156, 159; Aspects 14, 19, 21, 45, 84, 91, 93; HE 65; LJ 65-70; PI 65; RWV 67-68, 70; WAFT 64.

EMF always defends values of "culture and civilization." He is a "Humanist." He commits several "minor
heresies" against his "faith." These are easily illustrated in
his work. The first is "the Doctrine of the Great Refusal"
illustrated by Rickie [LJ]; and the "Noble Savage."

224. Macaulay, Rose. "E. M. Forster," in Living Writers:
     Being Critical Studies Broadcast in the BBC Third Pro-
     gramme, edited by Gilbert Phelps. London: Sylvan Press,
     1947, pp. 94-105.
        "Very few sensitive writers of his own or of later
generations can have escaped [his influence] altogether." He
is "the father of the twentieth century novel." There follows
a general appreciation of his work.

225. Marshall, Margaret. "Notes by the Way," Nation,
     CLXV (16 Aug 1947), 166.
        A review of Collect. Of all the tales, "The Road to
Colonus" and "The Eternal Moment" are the two that "endure
best and are of particular interest because they contain in
embryo the themes, symbols, and ideas" of EMF's novels.
The collection, however, is uneven in quality. "The Other
Side of the Hedge" is definitely a "failure."

226. "People Who Read and Write," New York Times Book
     Review, (29 June 1947), 8.
        EMF "looks very British: bony and angular." On his
first visit to the U.S. he noted that he "hadn't anticipated
[the] charm" of Americans. He likes Eudora Welty's stories
and finds Fitzgerald "puzzling, fascinating and possessing a
fine sense of mystery."

227. "Portrait," Saturday Review of Literature (NY), (13
     Sept 1947), 7.
        EMF has "probably set down the outline of [literary]
standards better than any other creative writer in history."

228. Prescott, Orville. "Outstanding Novels," Yale Review,
     NS XXXVII (Autumn 1947), 190.
        A review of Collect. "Artful, thoughtful, ironic
[but] ... these stories ... are too playful and slight to challenge serious comparison with [his] masterpiece, Passage to
India."

228A. Rago, Henry. "Aspects of the Novel," Commonweal,
      XLVI (2 May 1947), 73-74.
        A review of Aspects. Its opinions, though twenty

years old are still "fresh," probably because they are a matter of EMF's "own quite personal language." His position is "explicit."

229. Redman, Ben Ray. "New Editions," Saturday Review of
        Literature (NY), XXX (12 July 1947), 32.
            A review of Collect. "... it may be suggested that
some critics have mistaken Mr. Forster's remarkably smooth
writing for writing of an even superior kind and they have tried
to make his novels bear a weight of meaning for which, probably, they were not designed." EMF's tales, however, "have
acquired a new nostalgic quality" but none could possibly be
called "great." They have, nevertheless, varying degrees of
excellence.

230. "Tourist," New Yorker, XXIII (3 May 1947), 27-28.
            EMF is paying his first visit to the U.S. He is a
"shy, apprehensive Edwardian gentleman of sixty-eight." He
has come to address a symposium at Harvard on "The Raison
d'être of Criticism in the Arts." He noted that he is "somewhat detached" from his novels now. "Sometimes they don't
even seem like mine."

231. Watts, Richard. "Ironic Speculation," New Republic,
        CXVII (27 July 1947), 27.
            A review of Collect. The stories represent "virtual
artistic perfection. They are exquisitely wrought with grace,
deceptive ease and great felicity."

1948

232. Bentley, Phyllis. "The Novels of E. M. Forster,"
        College English, IX (April 1948), 349-356.
            A survey of the five novels. The author calls
WAFT "an astonishingly mature work for a young man of
twenty-six." RWV is a "charming, sunny novel"; HE is an
"enthralling story of personal relations" and PI is a "fine
achievement" in which EMF "brilliantly" expounds a humanistic creed. LJ is a fuller statement of the theme of "conflict between the true and the sham" than is RWV.

233. Brocklehurst, A. G. "The Short Stories of E. M.
        Forster," Manchester Literary Club. Papers, LXVII
        (1948-1949), 86-104.
            A review of Collect. The tales are told in "straightforward, and frequently beautiful prose." EMF does not

employ "the whip-crack ending," nor is he "much concerned
with neatness in anecdote."

234. Stewart, Douglas Alexander. The Flesh and the Spirit:
       An Outlook on Literature. Sydney, Australia: Angus and
       Robertson, 1948, pp. 17-24.
            PI is "a dramatization of the ultimate loneliness of
the spirit of man, its struggle for communion with its fel-
lows, its inevitable failure and its solitary exile." EMF is
"free from ideological rancour" and is "searching for human
truth."

235. Stringer, Arthur. Red Wine of Youth: A Life of Rupert
       Brooke. New York: Bobbs-Merrill, 1948. Index. p. 116.
            Brooke once stayed at a pensione in Florence where
he encountered EMF "characters." He found them "difficult
to live with."

236. Warren, Austin. A Rage for Order: Essays in Criti-
       cism. Chicago: University of Chicago Press, 1948,
       pp. 119-130.
            EMF's "double vision" allows him modulation from
"crisp comedy" to "a delicate path," passage from "prose to
poetry and back again." The peril of the gift results in his
not always being able to keep the two worlds in proper perspective. HE "fails certainly" because of that inability.
EMF's production has been sparse and he has no wide popularity, except for PI. He lacks power, but the deficiency is
felt only in retrospect.

                              1949

237. Boyle, Alexander. "Novels of E. M. Forster," Irish
       Monthly, LXXVIII (Sept 1950), 405-415.
            The purpose of the article is to suggest some of the
reasons for the popularity, in certain circles today, of EMF.
In him is reflected the dilemma of the novelist in the twentieth century.

238. Breit, Harvey. "E. M. Forster," in The Writer Ob-
       served. Cleveland and New York: World, 1949, pp. 53-56.
            EMF is "gentle and abstracted" and has revised
some of the positions he took in Aspects of the Novel, notably
that he now is "compelled" to recognize the "genius" of
James Joyce but, nevertheless, cannot "appreciate him."
George Eliot has "gone up" in his estimation. He likes the

writings of Katherine Anne Porter.

239. Breit, Harvey. "Talk with E. M. Forster," New York
      Times Book Review, (19 June 1949), 35.
            A rambling discussion of various topics during an
      interview. The writer dwells on EMF's first visit to a bur-
      lesque house.

240. Cecil, Lord David. "E. M. Forster," Atlantic,
      CLXXXIII (Jan 1949), 60-65.
            EMF is not a revolutionary author in the sense of
      Virginia Woolf. He is as didactic a writer as George Eliot.
      His work "pulses with intelligence and sensibility," but he
      does not make these elements his ultimate standards. When
      he draws the world, its moral aspects strike him most
      forcibly. He ranges people primarily in moral categories
      and the pattern he imposes is primarily that of his moral
      vision.

241. Cecil, Lord David. Poets and Story-Tellers. London:
      Constable, 1949, pp. 181-201.
            Essentially the same as #240.

242. Evans, B. Ifor. English Literature Between the Wars.
      London: Methuen, 1949, pp. 27-39.
            The influence of EMF throughout the period was "con-
      siderable." His "methods are new, but they are immediately
      intelligible." Despite the "brilliance of incident and dialogue"
      EMF remains a "moralist." He has a gift, "rarely possessed,"
      of "rhythmic prose."

243. Howe, Susanne. Novels of Empire. New York:
      Columbia University Press, 1949. Index. pp. 6, 11, 22, 33,
      34, 38, 54, 56, 71, 78, 80, 164.
            Fielding of PI is young Oakfield's [William Arnold,
      Oakfield, 1853] modern "blood brother." Both are "eternally
      twisting their heads to look forward and backward as well as
      all around ... both have charm and great courage."

244. Keynes, John Maynard. Two Memoirs: Dr. Melchior and
      My Early Beliefs. London: Hart-Davis, 1949.
            Passim references to Keynes' and EMF's friendship.

1950

245. Bowen, Elizabeth. "E. M. Forster," in Collected
     Impressions. New York: Knopf, 1950, pp. 119-126.
         WAFT contains in embryo all five of EMF's books.
They are written with "authority" and "power ... to expand
within the mind." Behind his irony and his impersonality,
he is "passionately civilized." The essay was reprinted from
the Spectator, 1936.

246. "Britten's New Opera: Libretto by E. M. Forster and
     Eric Crozier," Times (London), (14 Feb 1950), 2, col. 7.
         A note that EMF and Crozier are collaborating on a
libretto for Britten based on Melville's Moby Dick.

247. Brown, E[dward] K[illoran], "Rhythm in E. M. Forster's
     A Passage to India," in Rhythm in the Novel. Toronto,
     Canada: University of Toronto Press, 1950, pp. 87-115.
         The greatness of the novel is "dependent upon EMF's
mastery of expanding symbols and thematic structure, and on
that element in his spirit for which expanding symbols and
thematic structure are appropriate language."

248. "Degrees at Cambridge," Times (London), (9 June 1950),
     3, col 4.
         In honoring EMF at Cambridge, the orator at the
ceremonies, Mr. W. K. C. Gutherie, Fellow of Peterhouse,
noted that he "adorned everything he touched with the purity
and lucidity of his style."

249. Heilman, Robert Bechtold. Modern Short Stories: A
     Critical Anthology. New York: Harcourt Brace, 1950,
     pp. 306-311.
         A reprint of "Mr. Andrews" with a short commen-
tary. Heilman notes that, unlike Kafka, whose story is "the
harder," EMF employs traditional, mythical figures and concepts of which the general meaning is quickly apparent. But
he does not use them in a "conventional way"; he "rearranges
them sharply."

250. Savage, D. F. "E. M. Forster," in The Withered
     Branch: Six Studies in the Modern Novel. London: Eyre
     and Spottiswoode, 1950, pp. 44-69.
         EMF is an Edwardian novelist surviving into the
contemporary world as a public personality on the basis of a
past creativity. He is a "significant" writer whose work
proceeds from "an achieved center of being." That work

takes us to the "heart of the liberal dilemma."

251. Vines, Sherard. <u>One Hundred Years of English Liter-</u>
      <u>ature.</u> London: Gerald Duckworth, 1950. Index, pp. 127,
      129, 248, 256.
           EMF has the "art of not writing like a professional."
      RWV, HE, Celest, PI "illustrate [his] search for sweetness
      and light." His "satiric laughter is gentle in RWV; harsher
      in PI." His work is a "good example of the quarto presenta-
      tions which have pretty continuously replaced the Victorian
      folios."

      Warner, Rex. <u>E. M. Forster.</u> London: Longman's
      Green, 1950. See: #709.

1951

252. Ames, Alfred C. "New Forster Essays are Unhurried,"
      <u>Chicago Sunday Tribune, Magazine of Books,</u> (4 Nov 1951),
      12.
           A review of Two. The collection is an "important
      volume." Its greatest "lure" is its authorship. The essays
      are "spare, polished, unhurried, tense."

253. Beaumont, Ernest. "Mr. E. M. Forster's Strange
      Mystics," <u>Dublin Review,</u> CCXXV (Autumn 1951), 41-51.
           Behind EMF's social comedy there is the attempt to
      represent something that is "transcendental," especially in
      HE and PI. In both there are people who "know" something
      not known by their fellow characters. Both are women with
      "intuitive wisdom" and an "instructive" understanding. Their
      fascination for us lies in their "elusiveness."

254. Brower, Reuben A. "The Twilight of the Double Vision:
      Symbol and Irony in <u>A Passage to India,</u>" in <u>The Fields</u>
      <u>of Light.</u> New York: Oxford University Press, 1951.

255. Brooke, Jocelyn. "Four Cheers for Mr. Forster,"
      <u>Spectator</u> (London), CLXXXVII (9 Nov 1951), 609.
           A review of Two. EMF is "one of the great liber-
      ators, and as a novelist he has had influence primarily in
      the moral sphere." The book, however, "is greater than the
      sum of its parts." He is "always taking one off one's guard."

256. Chapin, Ruth. "Variety and Criticism," <u>Christian</u>
      <u>Science Monitor,</u> (21 Nov 1951), 11.

Review of Two.   Clearly observable in the collection
is "the phenomenon of the art and intellect both brilliantly and
positively in play." This was evident in AH and is now evident in Two.   The latter is, however, "tidier, romps less
both in its subject and style."

257.   Collins, Arthur Simons.   English Literature of the
       Twentieth Century. London: University Tutorial Press,
       1951. Index. pp. 3, 8, 10, 135, 184, 193-203, 218, 219,
       263, 288, 359, 368, 400, 403.
       EMF and D. H. Lawrence have much in common.
The "breakdown of the pre-1914 world becomes visible" with
their work. It was not until the 30's and the 40's that EMF's
"effect" was fully felt.   Basically, his "modernness consists in
the discomfort of soul" which made him a critic of contemporary civilization.

258.   Fremantle, Anne.   "Two Cheers for Democracy" (re-
       view), Commonweal, LV (9 Nov 1951), 126.
       One's first reaction to the volume is "to wish the
author hadn't been so remotely on the sidelines." EMF is "our
Montaigne." He is at his best when he is "most personal."
The book is as "astonishing as Archimedes, as supremely
detached as Aurelius."

259.   Gill, Brendon.   "Two Self-Portraits," New Yorker,
       XXVII (17 Nov 1951), 179.
       A review of Two. It would be "hard to think of any
other writer who gives one the impression of chatting face to
face with his readers." The volume is EMF's first "full-
length self-portrait since AH." That book "gave one the likeness of a student, middle-aged, frisky, and acute, whose subject ... was the moral nature of men and nations." EMF
will "live for his novels, not for his essays."

260.   Howe, Irving.   "Pleasures of Cultivation," New Repub-
       lic, CXXV (10 Dec 1951), 16-17.
       A review of Two. The reader immediately recog-
nizes in the essays EMF's traits of excellence, his freedom
from "stuffiness," and an assurance in dealing with the English
literary tradition, a readiness to converse on terms of intellectual equality, a shy humility, etc.

       Kettle, Arnold.   An Introduction to the English Novel.
       Vols. I and II. London: Hutchinson, 1951. See: 294.

261.   Krutch, Joseph Wood.   "In Defense of Values,"

Saturday Review of Literature (NY), XXXIV (1 Dec 1951), 25.

A review of Two. Though advertised as a "miscellaneous collection," the volume is unified more than usual in such collections of essays by the fact that EMF has a "very unified personality." His temperament as well as his opinions are commonly what is called "old-fashioned." He is "defender of values often overlooked and sometimes rejected by moderns."

262. Lancour, Harold. "Two Cheers for Democracy" (review), Library Journal, LXXVI (1 Nov 1951), 1801-1802.

The collection is a "pot-pourri" similar to AH. Except for the war-pieces, the essays "show their age unbecomingly." They meet the "high standard of Edwardian prose writing of which EMF is an acknowledged master."

263. Paulding, Gouverneur. "An E. M. Forster Miscellany, Generous and Civilized," New York Herald Tribune Books, (4 Nov 1951), 3.

A review of Two. A "fascinating collection and it shows how one civilized and generous spirit has managed to hold firm to the interests of civilization."

264. Porter, Katherine Anne. "E. M. Forster Speaks Out for the Things He Holds Dear," New York Times Book Review, (4 Nov 1951), 3.

A review of Two. The volume reflects an "admirable style--that is to say his own style, spare, unportentous, but serious." EMF is "an artist who lives in that constant state of grace which comes of knowing who he is, where he lives, what he feels and thinks about his world."

265. Pritchett, V[ictor] S[awdon]. "A Private Voice," New Statesman and Nation, XLII (3 Nov 1951), 496.

A review of Two. EMF is the "least moderate of men." He does not "believe in Belief." All his essays are touched by "that dislike of the will and intellect" noted by Trilling in his study. His essays display a "coolness, a hardness, sufficiency and maturity."

266. "A Qualified Tribute," Times Literary Supplement (London), (16 Nov 1951), 724.

A review of Two. The impact of reading the collection is something akin "to that of the novels, and in its total effect it is creative." It has "more deliberate unity than its predecessor" [AH].

267. Scott-James, R. A. Fifty Years of English Literature
      1900-1951. London: Longmans, Green, 1951. Index.
      pp. 34, 54, 66-71, 163.
            EMF is not among the "prophets" of the period.
WAFT has "none of the signs of maturity." LJ is "far more
ambitious, though not well constructed." RWV is "a perfectly constructed little comedy." HE exposes "the tragedy of
modern life." The "tragedy" of PI arises from the "com-
patibility of temperament" between the English and the Indians.

268. Shrapnel, Norman. "Mr. E. M. Forster," Manchester
      Guardian, (6 Nov 1951), 4.
            A review of Two. The title perfectly sums up EMF's
attitude. Too often, however, he goes "in for the deplorable
sort of overjauntiness that puts one in mind of the popular
parson who turns out to be a bit more popular than his flock."

269. Tait, Stephan and Kenneth Allott. A Room With a View.
      London: Arnold, 1951.
            A play adapted from the novel.

270. "Two Cheers for Democracy" (review), Booklist,
      XLVIII (15 Nov 1951), 97.
            "Miscellaneous essays, articles and broadcasts dat-
ing from 1936 ... [some] predominantly political in feeling
... [others] he has given ... ethical or esthetic treatment."

271. "Two Cheers for Democracy" (review), Bookmark, XI
      (Dec 1951), 57.
            The volume reflects "a distinguished English writer's
wise, civilized views of life and literature."

272. "Untidy Old Bird," Time, LVIII (19 Nov 1951), 118.
            A review of Two. "While demonstrating the range
of his mind, he also files a minority report on the direction
in which he thinks civilization is moving."

273. Zabel, Morton Dauwen. "The Trophies of the Mind,"
      Nation, CLXXIII (1 Dec 1951), 480.
            A review of Two. The "voice that speaks its relaxed
if sometimes deceptively amicable accents ... is still unmis-
takable. It remains one of the stubbornly honest voices of our
century." EMF is "the kind of artist who conceives of his art
as a mediator between art's rightful superiority to use and
the humanity that does not care about art at all."

1952

274. Ferry, David. "The Miracles of E. M. Forster,"
Harvard Advocate, CXXXVI (Dec 1952), 8-10, 34-35.
A discussion of how EMF "relates to reality" by
examining in the main, one novel, RWV, while "impudently"
ignoring other facets of his art.

275. "Forrest Reid Memorial," Times (London), (11 Oct
1952), 8, col. 2.
Yesterday [Friday 10 Oct] EMF presented to the
Lord Mayor of Belfast a plaque memorializing Forrest Reid,
the novelist. He attended a luncheon following the presentation.

276. Fuller, John. "E. M. Forster at Seventy," Adelphi,
XXVIII (Second Quarter 1952), 592-593.
EMF is the "strangest, the most persistent, the
most dominant reputation in contemporary literature." In
Two he speaks "more openly, more loudly than in any earlier
period of his life."

277. Hart-Davis, Rupert. Hugh Walpole: A Biography. New
York: Macmillan, 1952. Index. pp. 49, 59, 113, 255, 313.
Walpole liked LJ which he called a "very remarkable
novel." EMF, who had been sent the manuscript of Walpole's
The Wooden Horse, found it "good"; Walpole noted that EMF
"could put the rest of us [novelists] in his pocket." EMF
also praised Walpole's The Crystal Box.

278. Keir, W. A. S. " 'A Passage to India' Reconsidered,"
Cambridge Journal, V (April 1952), 426-435.
The purpose of the article is to approach PI as
"Forster wishes us to," as a work of art or an "impression,"
and only secondarily as "an argument or a political tract or a
social document." It is not to be read in "the hope of finding
in it either a clear cut and comprehensive 'philosophy,' or a
ready-made solution to the problems of its characters."

279. Leavis, F[rank] R[aymond]. "E. M. Forster," in
The Common Pursuit. London: Chatto and Windus,
1952. Reprinted from Scrutiny, VII (Sept 1938), 185-202.
The essay was also reprinted in The Importance of
Scrutiny: Selections from Scrutiny, A Quarterly Review,
1932-1948.
An essay-review of Rose Macaulay's The Writings of
E. M. Forster. Leavis notes that the problem with EMF is

the "oddly limited and uncertain quality of his distinction."
This is a problem not raised in the Macaulay volume. Her
book is a "guide, simply and chattily descriptive, to the not
very large corpus of EMF's works." The inequality in his
early novels is "extreme." He shows himself the born novelist in his comedy, but he is "almost unbelievably crude and
weak" when he aims at "making a poetic communication about
life."

280. Osgood, Charles Grosvenor. The Voice of England: A
      History of English Literature. New York: Harper and
      Bros., 1952. Index. pp. 592, 602, 607-608, 621.
           EMF's novels are "conservative in idiom and form."
They have a kinship with the English novel of manners; never-
theless, his work suggests a relationship with that of D. H.
Lawrence.

281. Porter, Katherine Anne. "E. M. Forster," in The
      Days Before. New York: Harcourt Brace. 1952, pp. 116-
      119.
           EMF is an artist "who lives in that constant state of
grace which comes from knowing who he is, where he lives,
what he feels and thinks about his world."

282. Warren, Austin. "E. M. Forster," in Aldridge, John
      W. (ed.) Critiques and Essays on Modern Fiction 1920-
      1951. New York: The Ronald Press, 1952. The essay
      originally appeared in American Review, (Summer 1937).
      It was reprinted as Chapter VIII of Warren's Rage for
      Order, q.v. #276.

                              1953

282A. Arvin, Newton. "A Private Secretary for the
       Maharajah," New York Times Book Review, LVIII
       (25 Oct 1953), 3, 49.
           A review of Hill. Though it does not throw any
"specially new light on EMF's literary powers [it] has at
least much of the interest, much of the novelistic liveliness
... that one would expect of any work of EMF's, however
secondary."

283. Borland, Alwyn. "James and Forster: The Morality
      of Class," Cambridge Journal, VI (Feb 1953), 259-280.
           The author compares James' The Princess Casamas-
sima and HE. Both treat of class from fairly disparate points

of view. There is, however, "more violence in Forster than in James." Both have received inadequate critical attention. Despite their points of contact "one does not spring from another."

284. Burlingham, Russell. *Forrest Reid: A Portrait and a Study*. London: Faber, 1953. Index. pp. 19, 30, 78, 158, 229, 237, 249; quoted 137, 208, 219, 219n; early story of 167; work and outlook compared with Reid's 165-7, 170.

In each of EMF's novels "moral issues are treated" and the characters "represent ideas which are greater than themselves." In Reid's works, however, the "scheme of moral values ... is rather different and less explicit." Morals in EMF's books are "less integrated into his art than inculcated by that art."

285. "Court Circular," *Times* (London), (14 Feb 1953), 8, col. 2.

EMF was honored by the Queen with an audience for the purpose of investing him with the Insignia of a Member of the Order of the Companions of Honor.

286. Downing, Robert. "Tolerance," *New York Times*, (15 March 1953), Sect. VI, 6, col. 5.

A letter in which the writer reacts negatively to EMF's essay of 22 February, "Tolerance." He can see no advance to brotherhood until the word "tolerance" is rooted "from the lexicon of international thinking."

287. Fraser, G. S. *The Modern Writer and His World*. London: André Deutsch, 1953. Index. pp. 90-95, 117, 138, 170, 173, 312.

EMF is the "most intelligent and sensitive, though not the most forceful or imaginative novelist writing [in the Edwardian period]. He has influenced such writers as L. P. Hartley and Christopher Isherwood. EMF is a "practical philosopher, interested in human behaviour in so far as it presents us with moral problems."

288. Fremantle, Anne. "A Civilization," *Commonweal*, LIX (4 Dec 1953), 232-234.

A review of Hill. "The astonishing achievement" of the book is the "3 D effect it continuously gives." EMF has "absolute pitch, the rarest of all gifts."

289. Fussell, Paul Jr. "E. M. Forster's Mrs. Moore:

Some Suggestions, " Philosophical Quarterly, XXXII (Oct
1953), 388-395.
        Into the character of Mrs. Moore has been fused
"the soul of Mrs. Wilcox" of HE, but also, Fussell believes,
some elements of the clairvoyante, Helena Petrovna Blavatsky
(1831-1891).

290.   Godden, Rumer. "The Eternal Charm of a Gilbert and
       Sullivan Kingdom in India, " New York Herald Tribune
       Book Review, (1 Nov 1953), 5.
               A review of Hill. The book can be called the
"shadow" of PI. "Like all shadows, it throws the substance
into stronger light; but it is remarkable on its own account. "
It "has very little life, but great depth and dignity. "

291.   "Hill of Devi" (review), Booklist, L (15 Nov 1953), 117.
               EMF "reports with humor and gentleness. " The book
"not only gives the reader an excellent opportunity to see how a
novelist incorporated his personal experiences into his art, but
also affords him a glimpse of a vanished way of life. "

292.   Hughes, Richard. "Mr. Forster's Quandary, " Spec-
       tator (London), CXCI (16 Oct 1953), 432.
               A review of Hill. Is the book a major work or a
"delicate trifle?" An author who publishes so little for so
long puts his public into a quandary. He can't be permitted
to publish a "potboiler. "

293.   Kapur, R. K. "The Other India, " New Republic, CXXIX
       (2 Nov 1953), 28.
               A review of Hill. The book is filled with "delicious
accounts of ... the thermopylisms of the Indians. "

294.   Kettle, Arnold. An Introduction to the English Novel,
       Vol. II: Henry James to the Present Day. London:
       Hutchinson's, 1953. Index. pp. 20, 63, 68, 86, 152-64,
       178, 184.
               EMF is not a writer of the stature of D. H. Law-
rence or James Joyce, but he is a "fine and enduring artist. "
PI is his most successful novel. WAFT is far less ambitious;
HE is quite as ambitious, but the "least satisfactory" of the
five novels.

295.   "Letters from India, " Times Literary Supplement
       (London), (16 Oct 1953), 654.
               A review of Hill. The book displays a "sensitive
understanding of the Indian mentality. " EMF has written

"nothing more sparkling, more gay, more imbued with delicious humour."

296. Liddell, Robert. Some Principles of Fiction. London:
Cape, 1953. Index. pp. 75, 97, 118, 139, 147; Aspects
115-116, 119; HE 98; LJ 37.
     Liddell notes that EMF said that the "novelist's
touch is bad in biography, for no human being is simple."
He discusses EMF's theory of the round and flat concept of
character.

297. Maclean, Hugh. "The Structure of A Passage to India,"
University of Toronto Quarterly, XXII (Jan 1953), 157-
171. Reprinted in Shahane, V. A. (ed). Perspectives
on EMF's A Passage to India. New York: Barnes and
Noble, 1968. pp. 19-34. See: #646.
     The discussion rests upon E. K. Brown's demonstra-
tion that there exists in PI an intricate symbolic pattern which
gives the novel its form. EMF's title, theme, and structure
are reflected in Whitman's poem, "Passage to India," but in
reverse. The poem's second section sets out EMF's three-
part division. The first two parts of the novel are almost
totally satire and offer no solution to the obstacles which prevent understanding. Nevertheless, the implication of the book
is like the poem, optimistic of the resolution of the difficulties.

298. McConkey, James R. "The Novels of E. M. Forster,"
Dissertation Abstracts, XII (1953), 811-812.
     The dissertation was published under the same title
by Cornell University Press, 1957. See: #387.

299. Magnus, John F. "Tolerance," New York Times,
(1 March 1953), Sect. VI, 4, col. 5.
     A letter in response to EMF's essay, "Tolerance,"
published 22 February. The correspondent suggests another
word, "toleration," which "came to stand specifically in
Britain for freedom of worship." The word also applies to
EMF's thesis.

300. Muehl, John Frederick. "Old Tyrannies Die," Saturday Review (NY), XXXVI (12 Dec 1953), 12.
     A review of Hill. The book is "both simple and a
complex" volume. It is an "historical microcosm in which
the collapse of a feudal regime is mirrored ... also a work
of art ... in the last sense ... a personal record."

301. "People and Events of the Week, and the New Year

Honours, " Illustrated London News, CCXXII (10 Jan 1953),
64.
        Notes the appointment of EMF as a Companion of
Honour.   There is also an indication that he is responsible
for the libretto, with Eric Crozier, of the opera, Billy Budd,
by Benjamin Britten.

302.   Plomer, William.   "Books in General, " New Statesman
        and Nation, NS. XLV (17 Oct 1953), 457-458.
                A review of Hill.   An "immensely entertaining and
effective" book.   EMF's "interspersed commentary" puts
"everything in perspective. "

303.   "Prince of India, " Newsweek, XLII (26 Oct 1953), 119.
        A review of Hill.   By basing his work on his own
writings when he was young, EMF has evaded the tragedy
into which many prominent writers fall when they produce
"genial reminiscences" less interesting than the books which
made them famous.

304.   Rau, Santha Rama.   "Tribute to Ghosts, " Nation,
        CLXXVII (14 Nov 1953), 408.
                A review of Hill.   The volume is an "emendated,
glossed, and enlarged diary" of the author's first months in
India (1912-1913) and of the India revisited in 1921, interspersed with letters.   In essence, however, it is a sketch
book for PI.   It is "remarkable and evocative" and, as the
raw material of a great novelist, it is of "enormous value and
interest. "

305.   "Recent Books: Mr. Forster in India, " Times (London),
        (17 October 1953), 9, col. 2.
                A review of Hill.   The volume can be read as an in-
teresting account of a vanishing age or as a sketch of a personal tragedy.   EMF is an extremely good letter-writer with
a mind open to every impression.

306.   Rolo, Charles J.   "A Passage to India, " Atlantic, CXCII
        (Nov 1953), 108.
                A review of Hill.   "Wonderfully good letters ...
shaped ... into a delightful book--a vivid amusing picture,
permeated with the grotesque, of a vanished civilization. "
Here "is a slice of experience" which was included in EMF's
masterpiece, PI.

307.   Simches, Raphael.   "Tolerance, " New York Times,
        (8 March 1953), Sect. VI, 6, col. 4.

A letter noting that EMF's definition of tolerance in the February 22 issue was "extremely provocative." The correspondent wonders how EMF can "define a noun by using its verb." Prejudice can be eliminated, the writer maintains, "only through education and brotherhood."

308. Spender, Stephen. "Movements and Influences in English Literature, 1927-1952," Books Abroad, XXVII (Winter 1953), 5-32.
   The theme of EMF's novels has been the "realization of individual values through personal relations." In all of his novels he assumes that the "economic basis of his middle class persons was unchallenged." The end of PI, however, suggests the English Empire may destroy the very values necessary to "develop individual values and personal relations."

309. Spender, Stephen. "Personal Relations and Public Powers," in The Creative Element: A Study of Vision, Despair and Orthodoxy Among Some Modern Writers. London: Hamish Hamilton, 1953, pp. 77-91.
   A study of EMF's ideas and work which concludes with the concept that "the almost ideal vision of human individuals, and relations between them, which burns through EMF's novels, is one which people may turn to the more passionately just because it is uncontaminated."

310. Strong, L. A. G. Personal Remarks. London: Peter Nevill, 1953, pp. 205-209.
   EMF is "deeply concerned with the injury to the undeveloped heart." He is a "wise, ironic, and compassionate spectator of life."

311. "Three British Authors Honored by the Queen," Publisher's Weekly, CLXIII (7 Feb 1953), 758.
   A note to the effect that the Order of Companions of Honour was conferred upon EMF by Queen Elizabeth II.

312. Walker, Gordon. "Hill of Devi" (review), Christian Science Monitor, (31 Dec 1953), 9.
   The book fails to give the reader the benefit of the author's usual brilliant literary style. But it does provide "a warm and intimate series of pictures ... of India."

313. White, Gertrude M. "A Passage to India: Analysis and Revaluation," Publications of the Modern Language Association, LXVIII (Sept 1953), 641-657. Reprinted in Shahane, V. A. (ed.) Perspectives on E. M. Forster's

A Passage to India, A Collection of Critical Essays.
New York: Barnes and Noble, 1968.   See #646.
          PI, the best of EMF's novels, was published in 1924,
and received instant recognition.   The years since have seen
it established as a modern classic.   Nevertheless, the most
important element, its dialectical pattern, has not yet been
fully and specifically recognized.   This lack has resulted in
confusion and obscurity.   The meaning and importance of its
theme has not yet been fully grasped.   An attentive reader
notes that EMF suggests more than he reveals and there is a
risk in translating these suggestions into explicit statements.
There exists, nevertheless, in the work a strong and subtle
dialectical pattern by means of which the author attempts to
bind social, psychological and philosophical levels into a
harmony and to relate the characters and events of the novel
to each other and to the idea of the whole.   The single theme
of the novel, "the search for the wholeness of truth," is developed in each book of the novel in somewhat different
terms and different levels.   The dominant idea of the work
comes from a poem by Whitman.   The three books: Mosque,
Caves, Temple, represent a kind of Hegelian Thesis-
Antithesis-Synthesis of the statement of the problem and two
opposing solutions.   Part I sets up the central problem of
separation; Part II sees the rout of the forces of reconciliation; Part III represents reconciliation on the human level,
the cancelling of the effects of the caves.

314.   Wood, Percy.   "An Era of Princely Pomp," Chicago
       Sunday Tribune, Magazine of Books, (1 Nov 1953), 5.
             A review of Hill.   The book is a "sympathetic
study."   It is a biographical memoir of the late ruler of
Dewas State Senior.   EMF shows a "matchless command of
language."

                              1954

315.   Allen, Walter.   The English Novel: A Short Critical
       History.   London: Phoenix House Ltd., 1954.   Index.
             EMF on Sterne and Virginia Woolf; on Scott, 112-113;
on Wuthering Heights, 188; on Meredith, 225; on Hardy, 236;
attitude to life, 319-323; a "tragic humanist" and his earlier
work, 321-323; HE and PI, 324-336; as a moralist, 326.

316.   Chaudhuri, Nirad C.   "Passage to and from India,"
       Encounter, (June 1954), 19-24.   Reprinted in Shahane,
       V. A., ed. Perspectives On a Passage to India.   New

York: Barnes and Noble: 1968.

PI has had, perhaps, an "even greater influence in British imperial politics than in English literature." From the beginning, the novel became a powerful weapon in the hands of anti-imperialists and was made to contribute its share to the end of British rule in India.

317. Hafley, James. The Glass Roof: Virginia Woolf as a Novelist. Berkeley and Los Angeles: University of California Press, 1954. Index. pp. 4, 8, 9, 34, 50, 89, 145-146, 173.

When Virginia Woolf spoke of the Edwardian novelists as "materialists," she did not have EMF in mind. Night and Day calls to mind certain of his novels and also Virginia Woolf's criticism of his method. Jacob's Room is not the "great deep novel," as EMF has said. There is an "interesting and not entirely superficial resemblance between To the Lighthouse and HE."

318. Hickley, Dennis. "Ou-boum and Verbum," Downside Review, LXXII (April 1954), 172-180.

EMF becomes a "microcosm of the tendencies of a whole epoch," i.e. the typical agnostic and humanistic position of the early twentieth century intellectuals. He penetrates more deeply into the implications of this viewpoint in PI. In it, especially in the experience of the cave, the characters, unknown to themselves, have their "first religious experience." The good they hear, which they interpret as "ou-boum" had, perhaps, really been the words "I AM."

319. Johnson, Elaine H. "The Intelligent Mr. E. M. Forster," Personalist, XXXV (Winter 1954), 50-58.

To the climate of "jingoism" and "violence" EMF stands irrevocably opposed. To apply one word to him one would have to use the word "intelligent." But his intelligence carries "limitations" with it. He often avoids "climactic scenes," giving us "effect rather than action." He never describes anything he hasn't personally experienced. He lacks "robustness," and can not create any sustained atmosphere of emotion. His emotions are limited "to the middle notes."

320. Johnstone, J. K. The Bloomsbury Group: A Study of E. M. Forster, Lytton Strachey, Virginia Woolf, and Their Circle. New York: Noonday Press, 1954. pp. 159-266 and scattered references. No Index.

A discussion of EMF's works and his relationships to

the Bloomsbury group. A general study of his "aesthetics" is
also included.

321.   Leach, Elsie. "Forster's A Passage to India, XXXVI,
       Explicator, XIII (November 1954), Item #13.
            The culminating events in Chapter XXXVI (Part III)
of PI concentrate, significantly, many of the themes and symbols of the novel.

322.   Mercier, Vivian. "Finding an Epicurean Basis for a
       Victorian Culture," Commonweal, LXI (15 Oct 1954), 42-
       43.
            A review of The Bloomsbury Group: A Study of
E. M. Forster, Lytton Strachey, Virginia Woolf and Their
Circle by J. K. Johnstone. See: #319. The Bloomsbury
group were "earnest Epicureans." They owed a great deal to
G. E. Moore. There is a problem in the book: the author
writes as if the only novelist Virginia Woolf had as a contemporary was EMF. There is a "meaty" chapter which
analyzes EMF's work.

323.   Moore, Harry T. The Intelligent Heart: The Story of
       D. H. Lawrence. New York: Farrar, Strauss and Young,
       1954. Index. pp. 183, 309, 443.
            D. H. Lawrence quarrelled with EMF though he felt
a tenderness for him. DHL called him a "man of strong soul."
Moore notes that EMF pronounced DHL "the greatest imaginative novelist of his generation."

324.   O'Connor, William Van. "A Visit with E. M. Forster,"
       Western Review (Rocky Mountain Review), XIX (Spring
       1954), 215-219.
            A record of their conversation with a note that EMF
disclaimed that his own fiction was indebted to Christopher
Fry's theory of fiction.

325.   Pickerel, Paul. "Hill of Devi" (review), Yale Review,
       NS XLIII (Winter 1954).
            "Delightful reading" but "its real value lies in the
opportunity it provides to see the kind of experience that lay
behind PI."

326.   Pritchett, V. S. "Books; Genius and Saint," New
       Yorker, XXIX (30 Jan 1954), 93-94+.
            A review of Hill. It is a "gracious piece of collage"
done by someone "who has brought the art of leaving out to a
high point of perfection."

327.   "Telegrams in Brief," Times (London), (26 June 1954),
     5, col. 4.
          The University of Leyden, on the occasion of the in-
ternational P. E. N. congress in the Netherlands, awarded an
honorary degree to EMF.

328.   Temple, Phyllis. "The Hill of Devi" (review), Amer-
     ica, XCII (2 October 1954), 20-21.
          The "youthful exuberance of the letters is balanced by
the measured pace of the commentary." The importance of
the book lies, principally, in the fact that EMF wrote it.

329.   Trevelyan, George Macaulay. Layman's Love of Let-
     ters. London: Longmans Green, 1954.
          Takes lengthy issue with EMF's condemnation of
Scott's novels in Aspects.

330.   "University News: Manchester," Times (London), (14
     May 1954), 8, col. 3.
          The degree of Honorary Doctor of Literature was
conferred on EMF by Manchester University, Wednesday,
12 May 1954.

331.   Voorhees, Richard J. "Novels of E. M. Forster,"
     South Atlantic Quarterly, LIII (Jan 1954), 89-99.
          One of the chief themes of the novels is the "critical
difference between the genuine and the spurious in human
personality." His novels are a "magnificent argument against
the psychological and moral barriers that separate men."

332.   Woolf, Virginia. A Writer's Diary. Edited by Leonard
     Woolf. New York: Harcourt Brace, 1954. Index. pp.
     11-12, 19, 20, 49, 52, 76, 79, 82, 91, 93, 99, 115,
     171, 172, 224, 234-236, 263, 270, 297, 325, 326, 327,
     328.
          EMF did not think the characters in Night and
Day "likable," nor did he care for those in Voyage Out. He
admired Mrs. Dalloway more than Jacob's Room. He felt
when he finished PI that it "was a failure." When he read
The Waves he felt the "sort of excitement" which comes when
one believes that one has read a "classic."

                                1955

333.   Allen, Glen O.   "Structure, Symbol and Theme in
     E. M. Forster's A Passage to India," Publications of

the Modern Language Association, LXX (Dec 1955), 934-954. Reprinted in Shahane, V. A., ed. Perspectives on E. M. Forster's A Passage to India. New York: Barnes and Noble, 1968.

The structure is built around the novel's three-fold division. The major symbolic structure rests in the Marabar Hills, the Caves, the sun, echoes, serpents, snakes, and worms. If the novel has a theme, it expresses some predication about the way life is or ought to be.

334. Allen, Walter. "Reassessment: Howards End," New Statesman and Nation, XLIX (19 March 1955), 407-408.

HE appears as the "quintessential Forster" because of the repetition throughout the novel of "only connect" and a "great many other things as well." WAFT, LJ, RWV are minor masterpieces because of their scale. HE has, however, taken on "classic stature." It sets out to illuminate not only the problems of personal relations but also the problems of the relations between the classes and the sexes. "It is meant as a microcosm of England."

334A. Benson, Alice R. "E. M. Forster's Dialectic: Howards End," Modern Fiction Studies, I (Nov 1955), 17-22.

EMF's concern for "personal relations" is "organized into a critique by means of the procedures of dialectic."

335. Blythe, Ronald. "Shelley, Plain," New Statesman, NS L (15 Oct 1955), 466+.

A discussion of the author's visit with EMF.

336. Brocklehurst, A. G. "E. M. Forster Looks Back," Manchester Literary Club. Papers, LXX (1955-1957), 75-86.

A review of MT. The volume is "a notable biography written in his own plain, straightforward style." It has the "authority and the poise of literature."

337. Brooks, Benjamin Gilbert. "Three English Novelists and the Pakistani Scene," in Crescent and Green: A Miscellany. London: Cassell, 1955. pp. 120-130.

EMF is "rather a deceptive writer"; at first Brooks felt that he had "written a work wonderful in its real understanding of India," but on closer inspection it is evident that he has not. Nevertheless, the pattern of PI is "more adult than Kipling's Kim."

338. Edel, Leon. The Modern Psychological Novel. New

York: Grove Press, 1955. (originally published as
The Psychological Novel, 1900-1950). Index. p. x.
   Edel notes that his essay takes up the novel where
EMF's Aspects leaves it.

339. Havighurst, Walter. "Symbolism and the Student,"
   College English, XVI (April 1955), 432-434.
   A discussion of "The Road from Colonus" as an il-
lustration of the author's understanding of a symbolic story.

340. Kronenberger, Louis. "Mr. Forster Pays a Debt,"
   Reporter, XV (6 Sept 1955), 54-56.
   A review of MT. It would be difficult to praise EMF's
approach too highly. The volume is a "small, quiet book by
a very distinguished writer." It is the kind of a book that
is the best proof of "true distinction."

341. Marshall, Kenneth B. "Irony in the Novels of EMF,"
   Dissertation Abstracts, XV (1955), 587-588.
   The purpose is to "investigate the nature and the effect of irony" in EMF's novels by examining the means he uses
to achieve these effects and how these effects "contribute to
the total aesthetic effect at which EMF aims."

342. O'Connor, William Van. "Toward a History of Bloomsbury," Southwest Review, XL (Winter 1955), 36-52.
   A discussion of the various attempts to record the
history and the development of the Bloomsbury group with passim references to EMF.

[343-351--No entries]

1956

352. Annan, Noel. "Honesty about an Aunt," Manchester
   Guardian, (25 May 1956), 4.
   A review of MT. Inevitably, there is more of EMF
than of his aunt in the book. It reveals the "milieu from
which he sprang and the families which he created." Battersea Rise and Howards End are similar because the former
possessed for the Thorntons what the latter held for EMF.
The biography is an "honest book."

353. "At Home in Battersea Rise," Times (London), (10
   May 1956), 15, col. 4.
   A review of MT. Though not obviously his purpose,

EMF has adopted "an unusual way to tell us something about
himself." Therefore, his book is "doubly interesting." In
generations to come, readers and students will approach the
book to discover something about the genius of EMF, but they
will also "stay to admire Marianne Thornton if they have any
feeling for character at all."

354.   "Books," New Yorker, XXII (1 Dec 1956), 238.
       A review of MT. More than a mere act of familial
piety, the book presents a "remarkable woman [who] deserves
the close and unsentimental scrutiny her great-nephew gives
her." MT will "survive as a major work in the Forster can-
non."

355.   Brown, Ivor.   "EMF's Great Aunt," New Republic,
       CXXXIV (28 May 1956), 17-19.
       A review of MT. EMF has "done honor" to his ma-
terial.   His own autobiographical section covers only a few
years.   The reviewer hopes that he will now extend it "with
a full treatment of his life."

356.   Chase, Mary Ellen.   "E. M. Forster Weaves a De-
       lightful Family Biography," New York Herald Tribune
       Books, (20 May 1956), 1.
       A review of MT. The book contains all the "reas-
suring and delightful features of his earlier works." But it
"differs ... in method and subject." It is a "rare" and
"completely charming book."

357.   Dunlea, William.   "E. M. Forster Homage to Another
       Time," Commonweal, LXIV (6 July 1956), 352.
       A review of MT. The book is a "handsome labor of
love." EMF is one of the "sanest critics alive."

358.   Eastman, Richard.   A Guide to the Novel.   San Fran-
       cisco: Chandler Publishing Co., 1956.   Index. pp. 193-
       194.
       Lists five works by EMF: RWV, HE, Celest, PI,
Eternal, and offers a short summary of the plot of PI.   He
concludes that a mystic element pervades the novel, suggest-
ing the real "passage to India" which may some day unite
the English and the Indians.

359.   "Goldsworthy Lowes Dickinson" (review), Wisconsin
       Library Bulletin, LII (Sept 1956), 214.
       "An engaging biography."

360. Halsband, Robert. "Literary Talk," Saturday Review
      (NY), XXXIX (18 Feb 1956), 52.
          A review of The Writer Observed by Harvey Breit.
The reviewer notes that Breit has the knack of telling, in his
"miniature profiles," something of the personalities of his
sitters as well as their literary ideas. EMF is "like a
spare, intelligent, ruffled heron" who sometimes throws off
a delightful mot."

361. Harvey, John.   "Imagination and Moral Theme in
      E. M. Forster's Longest Journey," Essays in Criticism,
      VI (Oct 1956), 418-433.
          The structural flaws and technical defects in LJ are
not "mere superficial blemishes" but are the inevitable cor-
relatives of a confused or inadequate vision of life" and,
by examining the book's form, an evaluation of its "substances"
and of "the experience being offered us can best be approached."

362. Hobson, Harold. "Mr. Forster and His Great Aunt,"
      Christian Science Monitor, (17 May 1956), 7.
          A review of MT. There are three reasons why MT
should "excite interest."   Though one of the foremost of
British writers, EMF's output is small.   MT is a "piece of
family biography."   The book gives a "different view of Victorian England."

363. Hoskins, Katherine.   "Forster's Act of Gratitude,"
      Nation (NY), CLXXXII (30 June 1956), 554-555.
          A review of MT. For admirers of EMF's novels,
there should be "considerable entertainment." The interest of
non-admirers "will get clogged and finally sag."

364. Hough, Graham. "Bachelor Aunt," Spectator, CXCIV
      (11 May 1956), 663.
          A review of MT. Not even EMF's "charming piety"
can cast much of a glow on his particularly uncharming character. His tone is "less than impeccable; it seems to suggest
a partial reconciliation with that high-minded communal bully-
ing which it was formerly his main business to project."

365. Lewis, Naomi.   "Aunt and Nephew," New Statesman
      and Nation, LI (12 May 1956), 534.
          A review of MT. What the book lacks for us is the
"quality of fiction." As the "tale" progresses, EMF becomes
increasingly less retiring and subdued.

366. "Maiden Aunt," Times Literary Supplement (London),

(11 May 1956), 282.
"An enthralling, witty and elegant narrative."

367.   "Marianne Thornton" (review), Bookmark, XV (June
       1956), 208.
       A "loving delineation" of EMF's great-aunt.

368.   "Marianne Thornton: A Domestic Biography, 1797-1887"
       (review), Booklist, LII (1 July 1956), 456.
       The volume is "significant as a reflection of 19th
century middle-class English culture."

369.   Mary William, Sister. "Marianne Thornton: A Domes-
       tic Biography, 1797-1887" (review), Best Sellers, XVI
       (1 Oct 1956), 228-229.
       It is truly a "domestic biography." At times, how-
ever, quotations from letters become "tedious and monotonous."
The book is a "very interesting way" to meet EMF.

370.   Melchiori, Giorgio. The Tightrope Walkers: Studies
       of Mannerism in Modern English Literature. London:
       Routledge and Kegan Paul, 1956. Index. p. 255.
       Notes that EMF's comments on T. S. Eliot's Four
Quartets "were perceptive."

371.   Moody, William Vaughn and Robert Moss Lovet. A
       History of English Literature. 7th edition. ed. by Fred
       B. Millet. New York: Scribner's, 1956. Index. pp.
       428, 440.
       The surface manner of EMF's novels is realistic, but
his impatience with realism is apparent in "his introduction
into his plots of sudden acts of violence or accidents and his
willful juxtaposition of a romantic figure and a realistic en-
vironment."

372.   Pendry, E. D. The New Feminism of English Fiction.
       Tokyo: Kenkyusha, 1956. Index. pp. 27, 66, 71, 82.
       "It cannot be denied that she [Virginia Woolf] was
partly inspired by the experiments ... of EMF." He has also
influenced Elizabeth Bowen and Rose Macaulay. He has had
a "profound effect" on modern women novelists and has "cap-
tured the very mystery and magneticism of matronhood in his
Mrs. Moore."

373.   "Portrait of a Family," Newsweek, XLVII (21 May 1956),
       120.
       A review of MT. The book is "noteworthy for

recapturing the high-minded enthusiasm for life possible to
the English gentility before Victorian moral corsetry became
fashionable. " It is "a finely documented family portrait in
perspective. "

374. Rolo, Charles J. "Period Piece, " Atlantic, CXCVII
      (June 1956).
         A review of MT. The book represents a "triumph of
artistry over subject matter. " EMF's narrative is "low-
keyed and leisurely. "

375. Scott-James, R. A. Fifty Years of English Literature
      1900-1950. London: Longmans Green, 1956. Index.
      pp. 66-71.
         EMF was versed in Greek poetry and the fanciful ele-
ment which appears so often in his work is the result of this
influence. He was not deeply moved by Shaw or Wells though
he would not have been inattentive to The Way of All Flesh.
Certainly Jane Austen was the English writer who gave him
the greatest pleasure. His earliest novel, WAFT, has none
of the signs of maturity. LJ is far more ambitious but not
well constructed. RWV is a perfectly constructed little
comedy. "Passion should believe itself irresistible" is its
theme. The tragedy of modern life is exposed in HE. The
tragedy of PI arises from the incompatibility of temperament
between the English and the Indians.

376. Swinnerton, Frank Arthur. Background with Chorus.
      London: Hutchinson, 1956. Index. pp. 107, 157, 160,
      169, 219.
         Passim references to EMF's fame and his involvement
in the New Weekly.

377. Tindall, William York. Forces in Modern British Lit-
      erature: 1885-1956. New York: Random House, 1956.
      Index. HE pp. 94-95, 290; LJ 95, 300; PI 62, 94, 95,
      96, 290-291; RWV 95; "Story of a Panic" 300; WAFT 95-
      96, 300; Symbolism 287, 290-291, 300.
         HE and PI are the most impressive statements of
EMF's themes; LJ is less successful; WAFT is the most nearly perfect of his early novels and his most Jamesian. "Story
of a Panic" is his most "Laurentian" story.

378. Trilling, Lionel. "The Great-Aunt of Mr. Forster, " in
      A Gathering of Fugitives. Boston: Beacon Press, 1956.
      pp. 1-11.
         MT "rings with the enchanted precision of a French
Exercise. "

379. Wagenknecht, Edward. "E. M. Forster Writes Vivid
     Biography of His Great-Aunt," Chicago Sunday Tribune,
     Magazine of Books, (20 May 1956), 2.
           EMF gives us as "vivid characters and as vivid a
     picture of the 19th century as can be found in any novel, and
     he writes quite as well as he could write if ever he were giv-
     ing us another novel."

380. Walbridge, Earl W. "Marianne Thornton" (review),
     Library Journal, LXXXI (1 June 1956), 1517-1518.
           An "endearing memoir."

381. Welty, Eudora. "The Thorntons Sit for a Family Por-
     trait," New York Times Book Review (27 May 1956), 5.
           A review of MT. "Our foremost writer of fiction is
     exactly who is needed to comprehend human beings who have
     been real as well as those who are going to be."

381A. Wilcox, Stewart C. "The Allegory of Forster's 'The
     Celestial Omnibus," Modern Fiction Studies, II (Winter
     1956-1957), 191-196.
           The theme is "the innocent and fresh imagination of
     childhood." Its allegorical plan, out of which this theme
     develops, however, is less easy to perceive than one might
     first suspect. The basis of the "allegorical cosmography" is
     the Homeric symbol of Achilles' shield.

382. Woodcock, George. "Piety and Peacocks," Saturday
     Review (NY), XXXIX (26 May 1956), 19.
           As a biographer, EMF has his merits. He delineates
     "delicate psychological development." He allows his people
     to speak for themselves. It is not, however, one of his "great
     books."

                              1957

383. "E. M. Forster," English Fiction in Transition, I
     (Fall-Winter 1957), 22.
           A bibliography of secondary materials consisting of
     five items: notations of three dissertation abstracts and two
     dissertations in progress.

384. Enright, D. J. "To the Lighthouse or to India?" in
     The Apothecary's Shop: Essays on Literature. London:
     Secker and Warburg, 1957. Index. pp. 168-186.
           An examination of To the Lighthouse and PI. The

author discovers that both "share the same scrupulous concern for sincerity in personal relationships." EMF is at his
best in the conclusion of PI, "neither cynic nor sentimental-
ist: one who believes in love, but doubts whether it will ever
quite drive out fear and hatred."

385. Lehmann, John, ed. The Craft of Letters in English,
      Boston: Houghton Mifflin, 1957. Index. pp. 6, 11, 25,
      34, 46, 52, 53, 179.
         Notes that EMF claimed that Lytton Strachey "revolu-
tionized" the art of biography.

386. Lynsky, Winifred. Reading Modern Fiction. New York:
      Scribner's, 1957.

387. McConkey, James. The Novels of E. M. Forster.
      Ithaca, New York: Cornell University Press, 1957.
         I. Introduction: It is remarkable how inadequate
the criticism of EMF is. Rose Macaulay's book is merely a
"graceful appreciation." Trilling's study interprets his work
as a kind of "guidebook for the modern liberal." Thereby, he
misses much of the essential matter of the novels. The portion of EMF's novels which treat of human relationships is not
difficult to analyze, but it is only a portion of his work. He
is also interested in "transcendent realities." The Forsterian
hero is "incomplete," a result of a dissassociation between
the character and his universe; he is not, however, a
"mystic." The "Forsterian voice" is an important element
in all of his novels. It is a point of view which focuses upon
the characters from the mid-point. The best method of com-
ing to critical terms with EMF is through a study of that voice
and of his symbols. The latter is the richest and most intricate aspect of his work and gives his novels an effect not
unlike music. The method which will be used to analyze his
work is to relate his theories to that work.
         II. People. None of EMF's major characters can be
liberated from their creator. Despite his dislike of it, he
uses a fixed point of view--that of the detached author. This
focus is the basis of all of his irony; it is essential to his
"double vision."
         Major Characters: Detachment and Incompletion.
EMF's insight into human relations is a result of his detachment from those relations. The same detachment is developed
by those characters who gain the author's insight--"those who
are most aware ... of truth." The greatest moments of his
figures, particularly his males, are moments of simultaneous
failure and achievement.

Major Characters: The Feminine Spirit. One characteristic of EMF's characters is a lack of passion and sexual fulfillment. A "religiosity" colors his major characters.
The visionaries and the protagonists are those whom he calls
"feminine" whether they be men or women. Femininity is a
quality which he believes transcends sexual distinction. The
movement of the feminine spirit is toward love for the whole
world. Vision is achieved by these characters through acceptance of self-denial and detachment (e.g. Mrs. Wilcox of
HE and Mrs. Moore of PI). Those opposing femininity are
represented by the Wilcoxes. The femininity of the protagonists has not been developed by EMF to the extent to which it
is to be found in the intuitive characters. The protagonists
sense, but often only obscurely, an "unseen and transcendent
reality" and have "the problem of relating this reality to the
material world." HE is an account of the triumph of the
feminine spirit when that spirit is "unhampered by problems
of a sexual nature."

Minor Characters. Questions of adjustment offer
them no problems. They have none of the double vision of the
major characters.

III. Fantasy and Prophecy. These two qualities involve a distortion since they require a "liberation" from the
"phenomenal world." The sense of "mythology" is the major
element of both. It is their "backdrop." Fantasy is the
"lower of the two."

The Search for a Mythology. EMF's need for a
"mythological referent" is obvious. His progression is from
fantasy to prophecy. He is prophetic only in his last novel,
PI. His most obvious use of the myth of pure fantasy is
found in his short stories. It is a myth of earth and of nature
based on classical myth. Earth and nature are cast as "redemptive agents." This concept is developed in all of his
novels before PI. In PI, he finds that earth can no longer
function as a unifying element because man has become an
alien on its surface.

Fantasy: Room With a View. To understand EMF
fully as a novelist requires an understanding of all of his
novels--his renunciation as well as development of themes.
The earliest statement of these themes is to be found in RWV.
It clearly invokes the "dieties of fantasy" but one senses a
"partial impatience" on the part of the author with the limitations of fantasy.

The Beginning of a Pattern: Where Angels Fear to
Tread. The novel is more satisfying and successful than
RWV because it is not written in the same "fantastic spirit."
WAFT, however, is concerned with the same basic issues.

It marks the "elementary stages" of a pattern which was more extensively developed in the later novels: fruition and fertility, incompletion and detachment.

The Divisions of Reality: The Longest Journey. The two spheres of reality which EMF treats of in later novels are first apparent in LJ. Ricky is conscious of a separation of reality into physical and transcendent realms and is thus faced with a problem more complex than those confronted by the protagonists in the short stories, RWV, and WAFT. Ricky must make a proper adjustment between the seen and unseen. The solution is to "trust in the integrated reality of the instinctional life."

Prophecy and the Forsterian Voice. The matter of voice becomes more relevant in HE for here EMF approaches prophecy. It is still more important in PI where it achieves the level of prophecy and places EMF among writers such as Dostoevsky, Melville, Brontë and D. H. Lawrence. His prophecy, however, is not as intense as Dostoevsky's, because EMF's prophecy is not found largely within the characters and also because EMF has "greater ambivalence toward reason."

The Movement Toward Prophecy: Howards End. In HE, the countryside may provide an opportunity for "connection among men." Ruth Wilcox becomes a "statement of the transcendent unity," but "neither a plausible human being nor a bearer of the true implications of voice." HE does not fully realize its prophetic potentialities because the "two commitments have been forced into closer partnership than EMF can give them."

The Prophetic Novel: A Passage to India. PI most fully achieves its potentialities partly because EMF is most keenly aware that the division does exist. Earth no longer supplies a link between man and the "transcendent unity." Fielding's detachment from human reality permits him achievements in the realm of personal relationships. These are possible because he has no roots and desires none. In Mrs. Moore's "negation" is her strength; she has "redemptive powers" after her death which suggest re-birth after exhaustion, birth through death, which is EMF's "philosophical position." In the attitudes EMF takes in PI can be seen the "thematic progression of his novels." It is "a progression from a complete trust in physical reality to the denial of it in the Marabar Cave." It is a progression marked by "redemptive characters" from Mr. Emerson to Gino, Wonham, Ruth Wilcox, and Godbole.

IV. Rhythm. EMF's novels depend for much of their effect upon the use of rhythm.

Room With a View and Where Angels Fear to Tread.
The use of rhythm is more pronounced in LJ, HE, and PI than
it is in RWV and WAFT because the former are concerned
with the relation between the seen and the unseen worlds.   In
RWV and WAFT, rhythm does not often assume the "propor-
tions of an expanding symbol." It usually appears as an
"aesthetic device." In these novels there is a "repetition of
phrasing" noted in the other three.   Only one recurring image
in RWV takes on the qualities of an expanding symbol: water.

The Longest Journey.   One of the recurring motifs in
the novel is "the fragility of human existence." Water, steam,
and sea suggest flux.   The Cadbury Rings, the Constellation
of Orion achieve "greater expansion." Chalk is a recurrent
token of the purity and vitality of the earth.   Any discussion
of the rhythmic imagery of LJ would be incomplete without
reference to the Roman road level-crossing which, with Orion
and the Rings, "constitute the most satisfying imagery in the
novel." The level-crossing "binds the novel together."

Howards End.   The theme of instability remains in HE
but emphasis is not given to the concept of life as "a bubble."
Human relations must stand up under a greater burden than
they have known in the past, but they can still hope for help
from the earth.   It can help by awakening man to the continuity and unity which it affords.   The Cadbury Rings, a symbol
of this continuity and unity in LJ, is replaced by the house in
HE.   The house and the Six Hills become recurrent, ever-
developing images in the novel to suggest the "mysterious
power of place." The "master image" of the whole novel,
however, is water.   The characters are all voyagers upon the
sea.   The novel thus becomes "a modern epic." The ultimate
destination of the voyagers is the house.   This destination,
however, is not revealed until the end.   One of the greatest
triumphs of the novel is the repetitive images associated
with HE.

Passage to India.   HE does not "achieve nearly the
degree of final liberation and expansion as PI does" because
the lesser expansion in HE relates to a "never-resolved
conflict between the detached position of the Forsterian voice
and the position of Margaret Schlegel actively engaged within
the world of human relations." In PI, the disparity is
acknowledged in the opening chapter.   The Marabar Hills represent the "most provocative image of all of EMF's novels."
He intends the emptiness of the caves to represent "the absolute Brahman" and the "echo to represent Mrs. Moore's
incomplete awareness of that absolute." The repetition of
the word "come" serves as one of the rhythmic devices in
the novel.   In the "cave symbology," EMF "binds the whole

novel together" in a manner "hardly short of the miraculous. "
His use of rhythm in this and earlier novels "to imply an
order beyond the phenomenal world" is a "kind of echo. " The
major factor in the expansion of PI lies in the "fact that, for
the first time, EMF has realized that his two commitments--
one to the world of humans, the other to the mid-point between
that reality and the transcendent reality beyond, can never be
brought fully and satisfactorily together.

388. McCormick, John, Catastrophe and Imagination.
      London and New York: Longmans, Green, 1957.

389. Nehls, Edward. D. H. Lawrence: A Composite
      Biography. Vol. I. Madison, Wis.: University of Wis-
      consin Press, 1957. Index. pp. 173-174, 265, 266, 267,
      269, 272, 273, 573, n. 83.
          Gives a short statement of EMF's friendship for DHL,
      e. g. "I never knew D. H. Lawrence well, " and passim refer-
      ences.

390. Oliver, Harold J. "E. M. Forster: The Early Novels, "
      Critique, I (Summer 1957), 15-31.
          The purpose of the essay is to suggest, contrary to
      Elizabeth Bowen's remark, that "there never seems to have
      been any early work" of EMF, that his development is very
      significant indeed, and that his first three novels are interest-
      ing partly because they are less convincing statements of the
      theme which is more subtlety treated in HE and PI and part-
      ly because they have many of the virtues of those later novels
      along with faults which EMF was later to learn to avoid.

391. Sanders, Charles Richard. Lytton Strachey: His Mind
      and His Art. New Haven: Yale University Press, 1957.
      Index. pp. 347-348, 383 n. 177.
          EMF came to Strachey's defense by answering
      Bertrand Russell's charge that Strachey "had degraded his
      ethics" and implying that Strachey was not great but merely
      "very eccentric. " EMF's letter answering Russell appeared
      in The Listener, XLIII (17 July 1932), 97-98.

392. Wilson, Angus. "A Conversation with E. M. Forster, "
      Encounter, IX (5 Nov 1957), 52-57.
          EMF speaks in "quick, little bursts of words which
      end, as it seems, inconclusively, and then he usually adds
      one or two words more, which ... are often the real core of
      what he is saying. " Additional remarks are made concerning
      EMF's work.

393. Zabel, Morton Dauwen. "E. M. Forster: The Trophies
      of the Mind, " in Craft and Character; Texts, Method and
      Vocation in Modern Fiction. New York: Viking, 1957.
      pp. 228-252.
          EMF is a "liberal who admits the law of necessity, "
      and it has always been his forte to reconcile two tendencies
      which he sees in the writing of our century: "the popular ...
      and the esoteric. "

394. Zwerdling, Alexander. "The Novels of E. M. Forster, "
      Twentieth Century Literature, II (Jan 1957), 171-181.
          EMF's first three novels: WAFT, LJ, RWV, are
      novels of "morals and novels of manners. " HE strikes us by
      its "greater maturity and firmer control. " It has "found the
      maturity to question its own values, " unlike the earlier vol-
      umes. It "foreshadows the disillusionment" of PI. Its theme
      is "the disenchantment with the power of human relationships. "
      PI articulates the theme which had been "tenuously and almost
      surreptitiously developed" in HE.

                                1958

395. Aldridge, John. After the Lost Generation. New York:
      Noonday Press, 1958. Index. p. 216.
          When EMF wrote PI, it was beginning to be no long-
      er possible that the novelist could take for granted that his
      audience would understand his view of life. Yet, he was able
      to infuse his novel with a significance that transcended the
      specific characters and situations about which he wrote.

396. "Appeal to Nuclear Powers; 'Disaster' if Geneva Talks
      Fail, " Times (London), (31 Oct 1958), 7, col. 1.
          EMF was one among many prominent individuals who
      signed an appeal to the nuclear Powers noting that failure to
      agree at the Geneva talks on the suspension of tests would be
      a disaster.

397. "Britons Decry Soviet Action, " New York Times, (30
      Oct 1958), 3, col. 1.
          Notes that EMF among other prominent British au-
      thors protested the Soviet Union's action with regard to Boris
      Pasternak's winning the Nobel Prize for Literature.

398. Daiches, David. The Present Age in British Literature.
      Bloomington and London: Indiana University Press, 1958.
      Index. pp. 260-261.

A rather concise bibliography of EMF's works with
a notation that he occupies a place as a "minor classic
among English novelists. "

399. "E. M. Forster," English Fiction in Transition, I
     (Spring-Summer 1958).
     A bibliography of five secondary works.

400. Furbank, P. N. and F. J. H. Haskell, "E. M. For-
     ster" (interview), in Cowley, Malcolm, ed. Writers at
     Work: The Paris Review Interviews. New York:
     Viking, 1958. pp. 23-35.
         EMF's manner is firm, precise, yet none the less
     elusive. The questions asked range from the unfinished novel,
     Arctic Summer, to the method of writing novels, to specific
     questions about each of the five novels.

401. Hall, James. "Forster's Family Reunions," ELH, XXV
     (March 1958), 60-78.
         Most critics of EMF have made a great deal of his
     "liberalism, " but unlike Eliot (whose work gives title to the
     essay), a conservative who distrusted "a return to family
     roots, " EMF in every novel but one uses a "sense of family"
     to make "reconciliation with the adult world possible. " In
     each of those books "a conservatism about the family sustains
     his liberalism about institutions. "

402. Hoggart, Richard. "The Unsuspected Audience, "
     New Statesman and Nation, LVI (6 Sept 1958), 308-310.
         A British reader is unlikely to feel alien to PI even
     though he belongs to a different class, but he will feel a "bit
     outside" of the experience.

403. "Installation of Lord Adrian: Leicester University
     Chancellor, " Times (London), (21 June 1958), 8, col. 7.
         A note that, at the installation, EMF received the
     Honorary Degree of Doctor of Letters.

404. Kain, Richard M. "Vision and Discovery in E. M.
     Forster's A Passage to India, " in Charles Shapiro, ed.
     Twelve Original Essays on Great English Novels.
     Detroit: Wayne State University Press, 1958. pp. 253-
     275.

405. Kermode, Frank. "Mr. E. M. Forster as a Sym-
     bolist, " Listener, LIX (2 Jan 1958), 17-18. Reprinted
     as "The One Orderly Product, " in Puzzles and Epipha-

nies: Essays and Reviews 1958-1961. New York: Chilmark
Press, 1962. Reprinted in Malcolm Bradbury, ed. Forster:
A Collection of Critical Essays, Englewood Cliffs, New Jer-
sey: Prentice-Hall, 1966.
        EMF is a "kind of Symbolist." He declares for the
autonomy of art, for meaning and form as a "co-essence,"
for art as "organic and free from dead matter," for music
as the criterion for "formal purity," for the essential
anonymity of art. He believes that the novel must bring
about unity from "differentiation" in order to "find meaning."
These qualities are "Symbolist." Nevertheless, there are
qualifications to be made. He insists on the novel telling a
story. He believes that "organic" unity must be produced by
a process he calls "faking."

406. Klingopulos, G. D. "E. M. Forster's Sense of His-
        tory: and Cavafy," Essays in Criticism, VIII (April
        1958), 156-165.
        To ignore EMF's essay on Cavafy at the end of PP
is to do EMF a "serious injustice." There is good reason to
believe that EMF found in Cavafy a "stimulating influence
and ever a source of strength." There is room for an attempt
to relate his immediate sympathy with Cavafy to the rest of his
development, especially that which led to PI.

407. Leary, Lewis, ed. Contemporary Literary Scholarship:
        A Critical Review. New York: Appleton-Century-Crofts,
        1958. Index. pp. 191, 194, 273, 440.
        Indicates and evaluates several critical studies of
EMF.

408. McConkey, James. "The Voice of the Writer,"
        University of Kansas City Review, XXV (Winter 1958),
        83-90.
        Reference is made to Aspects with regard to the
"primitive voice found in all strong narrative." It is only in
PI that EMF "becomes fully aware of the problems which his
voice has occasioned him." In the novel he is aware of the
differences between "certain major accents of his voice" and
his "conscious commitment to personal relations." The
novel, however, "attempts no reconciliation."

409. Pritchett, V. S. "Mr. Forster's New Year," New
        Statesman, NS. LVI (27 Dec 1958), 912.
        EMF has survived as a novelist by "interposing,"
not by "imposing," and not by "sheer efficiency and man-
power" as have other novelists. His "interposition" has been

done by a "misleading slackness, by the refusal to speak in a public voice. " As a consequence, "the personal" has a "startling strength. "

410. Raleigh, John Henry. "Victorian Morals and the Modern Novel, " Partisan Review, XXV (Spring 1958), 241-264.
  EMF's novels are "filled with Butlerian echoes and attitudes. " LJ is a "repetition" of the "Butlerian thesis that the intellect is not supreme" and that "only common sense and instinct can make existence bearable. "

411. "Televised Version of E. M. Forster's Novel: Conflict of Generations Lost, " Times (London), (3 July 1958), 5, col. 5.
  A note that a dramatized version of RWV by Tait and Allott was presented 2 July. In this version, Lucy's doubts "seemed to be unnecessary, her self-questioning artificial. "

412. Toynbee, Philip. "E. M. Forster at 80, " Observer (London), (20 Dec 1958), 8, 10.

413. "University News--Leicester, " Times (London), (11 Jan 1958), 8, col. 4.
  A note to the effect that the title of Doctor of Letters was awarded to EMF by the University.

1959

414. Belvin, Betty June McLain. "Expanding Themes in the Novels of E. M. Forster, " Dissertation Abstracts, XIX (1959), 2610-2611.
  EMF acknowledges the importance of stylistic devices which can be grouped under the term "expanding themes. " This term he uses to refer to the "rhythmic opening out" of the great novels. The novels are then examined within the context of expanding themes.

415. Brown, E. K. "Revival of E. M. Forster, " in O'Connor, William Van. Forms of Modern Fiction. Bloomington, Ind.: Indiana University Press, 1959. pp. 161-174. Reprinted from The Yale Review, 1944. See #194.

416. Crews, Frederick C. "The Longest Journey and the Perils of Humanism, " ELH, XXVI (Dec 1959), 575-596.

Reprinted as Chapter V in E. M. Forster: The Perils
of Humanism. Princeton: Princeton University Press,
1962. q.v. #485.

417. "Friends Honour Mr. E. M. Forster: Luncheon at
King's College," Times (London), (10 Jan 1959), 8, col.
5.
    A luncheon was given honoring EMF on his eightieth
birthday. He was named as "the greatest living King's man."

418. Gerber, Helmut, ed. "E. M. Forster: An Annotated
Checklist of Writings About Him," English Fiction in
Translation, II (1959), 4-27.

419. Gransden, K. W. "E. M. Forster at 80," Encounter,
XII (Jan 1959), 77-81.
    In EMF's books, "the element of surprise does much
to keep things continually alive." He has "fought shy of making general pronouncements outside of his books." WAFT is
slight, "almost ... a libretto--but its structure reverberates,
towards the end, with the famous Forsterian echo." Much of
his work "seems to reflect the classical division of man into
the rational part and the animal part." RWV is "charming
and curious." HE is the "most elaborate of his novels."
PI is undoubtedly his "masterpiece."

420. Green, Peter. Kenneth Grahame: A Biography.
Cleveland and New York: World, 1959.
    Notes that EMF's use of Pan in his short stories
as "the emblem of Anti-Science as well as Anti-Calvin" belongs
to an unbroken tradition from Coleridge and Wordsworth through
Keats, Shelley, Arnold, the Brownings, Swinburne, Stevenson,
Brooke, and Saki.

421. Grubb, Frederick. "Homage to E. M. Forster," Contemporary Review, CXCV (Jan 1959), 20-23.
    EMF's latest book, MT, reaffirms a "motif operative
in his novels," that of "continuity and renewal rooted in the
life of nature and of family." He is a "gentleman of letters"
and a "great man." To him, good writing is a "morality" and
an interest in ideas and art is a way of life rather than a
career. His longevity affirms that "liberal values may survive
and triumph."

422. Jones, David. "E. M. Forster on His Life and His
Books," Listener, LXI (1 Jan 1959), 11-12.
    Jones speaks of EMF's connection with Cambridge.

EMF likes LJ best, and gets a "little bored" with HE. He still enjoys RWV and WAFT, however, because he still enjoys Italy. EMF is delighted with the success of PI. He is greatly influenced by Jane Austen.

422A. "King's Messenger, " Times (London), (1 Jan 1959), 9, col. 3.
    An editorial on EMF's birthday in appreciation of his contributions as a novelist, noting that a large measure of his success is due to the fact that EMF is "also a musician."

423. Lee, Lawrence Lynn. "The Moral Themes of E. M. Forster, " Dissertation Abstracts, XX (1959), 1790-1791.
    EMF has two major themes: one should be an individual and not just a social being; and men must love one another if they are to be men. These he "never gives up." A third theme: the power of the earth to save man, he later almost completely abandons.

424. McDowell, Frederick P. W. "Mild, Intellectual Light: Idea and Theme in Howards End, " Publications of the Modern Language Association, LXXIV (Sept 1959), 453-463.
    In HE, EMF expands the "deliberate analysis of highly complex social, moral, and political issues" begun in LJ. He has a conviction that "the enlightened imagination must continually modulate the inner and the outer lives." Margaret Schlegel has learned, and at the end of the novel continues to learn, how to "control the intelligible ends, the vagaries of impulse." McDowell's analysis of HE is "less directly political and social than Trilling's and less concerned with the problems of the intellectual as he self-consciously faces his society."

425. "Masefield's New Epic: The Story of Ossian, " Times (London), (23 April 1959), 6, col. 4.
    The last paragraph of the article is a note to the effect that two recorded readings by EMF have been issued (RG 153). He reads "Road to Colonus" and "What I Believe" in "a dry but youthful voice."

426. Panter-Downes, Mollie. "Kingsman, " New Yorker, XXV (19 September 1959), 51-86.
    A notation of EMF's eightieth birthday and the festivities honoring him at Cambridge. Included is a review of his life as a Fellow at King's College, Cambridge, and his work.

427. Pedersen, Glenn. "Forster's Symbolic Form," Kenyon
      Review, XXI (Spring 1959), 231-249.
              EMF "creatively encircles" the literal structure of PI
      with "symbolic form." As Adela's passage to India reveals the
      "absence of form on the literal level," so Mrs. Moore reveals
      the presence of form on the symbolic level. Where there is
      no form, there is no morality; where form is, there is im-
      mortality.

428. Randles, W. G. L. "The Symbols of the Sacred in
      E. M. Forster's Howards End," Revista da Faculdade de
      Letras (University of Lisbon), Ser. III, 3 (1959), 89-102.
              The purpose of the article is to "explain" HE in the
      terms commonly used by the historian of comparative religion.
      Though permeated by the spiritual, EMF's world is not re-
      ligious. He attempts "the manifestations of the spiritual" but
      refuses to grant them a "system."

429. "Social News," Times (London), (1 Jan 1959), 10, col.
      1.
              A note that EMF is "80 today."

430. Spence, Jonathan. "E. M. Forster at 80," New Re-
      public, CXLI (5 Oct 1959), 17-21.
              EMF is in "constant danger of over-simplification or
      misrepresentation." In the most effective of his short stories
      ("Road to Colonus," "The Machine Stops"), as in WAFT and
      RWV, "nearly every character can be typed by a quotation,"
      but in LF and HE EMF's treatment of character "has de-
      veloped in breadth and complexity."

                                1960

431. Crews, Frederick C. "E. M. Forster, An Historical
      and Critical Study," Dissertation Abstracts, XIX (1960),
      2951.
              A "systematic effort to set forth the dominant beliefs
      and loyalties" of EMF and to place these in an historical per-
      spective. Finally, the work attempts to bring this knowledge
      to bear upon a critical examination of his longer fiction.

432. Crews, Frederick C. "The Limitations of Mythology,"
      Comparative Literature, XII (Spring 1960), 97-112. Re-
      printed as Chap. IX in E. M. Forster: The Perils of
      Humanism. Princeton: Princeton University Press,
      1962. See: #485.

433. "Forster Ms. Brings $18,200 in London," New York
      Times, (23 June 1960), 3, col. 3.
          Lew Feldman, a New York book dealer, bought the
draft autograph manuscript of PI at a sale for the benefit of
the London Library. He paid £6,000 ($18,200). A spokes-
man for Christie's, the London gallery at which it was sold,
noted that the price was the highest ever paid for a manuscript by a living author.

434. Hale, Nancy. "A Passage to Relationship," Antioch
      Review, XXI (Spring 1960), 19-30.
          No larger theme has been attempted in the novel of
time than that of PI. It is the theme of separateness, division; so obviously the cause of all of our woes, so apparently
irredeemable. PI is concerned not only with relationships
but with the subject of relationships.

435. "Head of Theatre Guild Sees Forster Play." Times
      (London), (9 March 1960), 4, col. 1.
          A note that Lawrence Langner, head of the Theatre
Guild of America, flew to Oxford after a telegram from his
daughter suggested that he do so, to see the Rau adaptation of
PI. The New York Times reported that he planned to buy the
play, but knowledge of the plans was denied.

436. Hoy, Cyrus. "Forster's Metaphysical Novel," Publi-
      cations of the Modern Language Association, LXXV
      (March 1960), 126-136.
          HE can be treated as a metaphysical novel because
it is concerned with metaphysical problems. These are im-
plicit in the clash of motive and purpose.

437. Karl, Frederick R. A Reader's Guide to Joseph Con-
      rad. New York: Noonday Press, 1960. Index. pp. 55,
      158.
          Mrs. Gould (Nostromo) is a "forerunner" of Mrs.
Wilcox (HE) and Mrs. Moore (PI).

438. McDowell, Frederick P. W. "Forster's Many Faceted
      Universe: Idea and Paradox in The Longest Journey,"
      Critique, IV (Fall-Winter 1960-1961), 41-63.
          Though faulty, LJ is possibly the most provocative
of EMF's books. It illustrates the virtues of its defects and
has "much intellectual substance." It "represents an advance
in subtlety and complication over RWV and WAFT." Though
EMF's artistry is better in HE and PI, "the depth, the scope,
and the flexibility of [his] literary intelligence and his pas-

sionate devotion to the life of the mind and spirit [are] most
directly in LJ."

439. Oliver, Harold J. The Art of E. M. Forster. Mel-
    bourne (Australia): Melbourne University Press, 1960.
        The main concern of the volume is with EMF's fic-
tion and most particularly his novels. There is no separate
consideration of AH, Two, GLD, PP, Hill, Alex. Oliver
notes that there have been "at least three other book-length
studies" of EMF, the "best of which is Trilling's." He feels,
however, that Trilling's can "be sometimes corrected" and
"more often supplemented in matters of interpretation."
        Oliver treats of EMF's subject and method, his
minor fiction, HE, PI; he notes that EMF's influence may
have "skipped a generation." There is a "greater similarity
to his style and outlook among the novelists writing in the
'40's and 50's" than among those in the generation which succeeded him. Some of the novelists influenced by EMF are
P. H. Newby, C. P. Snow, and Angus Wilson.

440. "A Passage to India by no Means a Novelist's Play,"
    Times (London), (20 Jan 1960), 6, col. 2.
        A review of the Rau adaptation of PI. The novel
lends itself more readily to the stage than does RWV because
it is less a "creative imagination than a deliberate appreciation of the workings of a society living under alien rule."
Miss Rau accepts unreservedly the novelist's view of India.

441. "Passage to the Stage," Time, LXXV (1 Feb 1960),
    53.
        A review of the Rau adaptation of PI. Doing a stage
version of PI is akin to trying to rewrite the Bhagavad-Gita
as a sonnet. Although the adapter had to leave out much of
the novel, she managed to "extract the center without damag-
ing the heart."

442. "Photograph," Times (London), (9 Jan 1960), 14.
        A photograph of EMF and Mukul Day with a sample
of the latter's art and a note that EMF opened an exhibition of
Day's work at the Commonwealth Institute, South Kensington,
8 Jan. 1960.

443. Raina, M. L. "Traditional Symbolism and Forster's
    A Passage to India," Notes and Queries, NS. XIII (Nov
    1960), 416-417.
        The relevance of EMF's division of the novel into
Mosque, Caves, Temple to the traditional symbolism of the

Indian year has not as yet been noted. In Indian myth, the seasons of the year correspond to the dissipation and restoration of order.

444. Panter-Downes, Mollie. "Letter From London," New Yorker, XXXVI (14 May 1960), 184-185.
A review of the Rau adaptation of PI. The play is "one of those rare dramatizations of novels which give almost complete satisfaction to everyone."

445. Seward, Barbara. The Symbolic Rose. New York: Columbia University, 1960. Index. pp. 131-132.
In LJ, EMF uses a "significant rose" to convey certain of his basic ideas. It is created by Stephen (near the end of the novel) out of burning paper. It symbolizes to Rickie the reality he has sought in humanity, literature, his wife, and the memory of his mother.

446. "Smooth Passage to India," Times (London), (21 April 1960), 16, col. 3.
The article notes that, since the presentation of the play at Oxford, roughnesses in production have been smoothed away and the performance at the Comedy "reflects cleanly and excitingly a remarkably sensitive and beautiful rendering of the novel."

447. "Social News," Times (London), (1 Jan 1960), 12, col. 1.
A note that EMF is "81 today."

447A. "Social News," Times (London), (31 Dec 1960), 10, col. 2.
A note that EMF will be 82 tomorrow [Sunday, Jan 1961].

448. Wilson, Harris, ed. Arnold Bennett and H. G. Wells: A Record of a Personal and a Literary Friendship. London: Rupert Hart-Davis, 1960. Index. p. 20.
Of all the novelists of "restricted popularity" at the time, only Conrad, James, and Forster have retained the "substantial respect of critics."

1961

449. Austin, Don. "The Problem of Continuity in Three Novels of E. M. Forster," Modern Fiction Studies, VII (Autumn 1961) 217-228.

The problem of continuity is central in LJ, RWV, WAFT and is associated with family. Life continues in so far as the family continues, and for the family to continue a reconciliation of the past and the present is necessary.

450. "Authors Awarded New Honour," Times (London), (11 May 1961), 9, col. 3.
EMF was among five authors who had conferred upon them Companionships of Literature by the Royal Society of Literature. He was, however, not present for the presentation of the scroll. It was accepted by his cousin, Philip Whicelow.

451. Barnett, Sylvan, Morton Berman, William Burto. An Introduction to Literature. Boston: Little, Brown, 1961. Index. pp. 15, 41.
Passim reference to Aspects.

452. Beebe, Maurice and Joseph Brogunier, "Criticism of E. M. Forster: a Selected Checklist," Modern Fiction Studies, VII (Autumn 1961), 284-292.

453. Boyle, Ted E. "Adela Quested's Delusion: The Failure of Rationalism in A Passage to India," College English, XXVI (March 1961), 478-480.
When Adela declares to Fielding that Aziz has not assaulted her and adds that she has had an hallucination, EMF offers an insight into the larger theme of the novel--the failure of untempered rationalism to destroy the barriers which isolate men. In order for Adela to fulfill herself, she must strike a balance between the intellect and the emotions; so too, EMF says, must all men.

454. Dauner, Louise, "What Happened in the Cave? Reflections on A Passage to India," Modern Fiction Studies, VII (Autumn 1961), 258-270. Reprinted in Shahane, V. A., ed. Perspectives on E. M. Forster's A Passage to India. New York: Barnes and Noble, 1968.
Though EMF's most popular novel, PI leaves the reader with a "vague sense of frustration." He is elusive sometimes because of subtlety, sometimes through "infirm control of structure," and notably through "inability to seize upon and fully realize the potentials of an archetypal symbol," the Marabar Caves. Though interpretations of them are diverse, this article examines them as natural phenomena or nature symbols, and as archetypes or psychological symbols. The Caves are a setting for irrational experience and are arche-

typal. Archeologists have uncovered evidence that caves have
functioned in the most critical events in the life of early man
and have been identified with the concepts of unity and of a belief in an aspect of the spiritual. Though, on the surface, the
novel is one of "barriers," its underlying life carries the implications of unity. The cave, then, because of its long as-
sociations in the history of man with unity, is, as EMF implies, the only real solution to the problem of disunity. But,
because the cave in man's history has been also associated with
a place of burial, it also carries the meaning of death and
separation. These are also themes in PI. The cave is thematic in its implication of good-and-evil and can be explored
and dramatized only through a series of "variations." The
cave, in man's primitive life, was also considered as the
"site of divine power, the Mother, or female potency, the
place of initiation into adulthood, a symbol of maturity, of the
future, of rebirth and resurrection." Adela's experience in
the cave is, therefore, ambivalent, having subjective and objective meanings. It reveals to her her own limitations and
objectively it poses Western rationality against Eastern mysticism, the conscious against the unconscious.

455.   "E. M. Forster Has Attack," New York Times (11
       April 1961), 31, col. 2.
       A report of a "slight heart attack" suffered by EMF
and a report that he is "quite comfortable" in a hospital. His
age is noted as eighty-one.

456.   Ford, Boris, ed.   The Pelican Guide to English Litera-
       ture, Vol. VII: The Modern Age.   Baltimore: Penguin
       Books, 1961.   Index. pp. 14, 21, 26-27, 74, 75, 197,
       210, 228, 229, 245-256, 257, 260, 261, 266, 268, 473,
       522; Aspects, 250, 257; "Curate's Friend," 248; HE,
       254, 266; LJ, 249-250, 254; "The Machine Stops," 248;
       MT, 247; PI, 26, 74, 251, 254-256, 261; RWV, 253;
       "Story of a Panic," 248; Two, 260, 268; "What I Believe,"
       27.

457.   Garnett, David.   "Some Writers I Have Known:
       Galsworthy, Forster, Moore, and Wells," Texas Quarter-
       ly (University of Texas), IV (Autumn 1961), 190-202.
       EMF is "always drawing clear, sharp distinctions
between people and drawing them in unexpected places. He
has great humour." Both EMF and Galsworthy appealed to the
English intelligentsia and both were liked because they at-
tacked British complacency, smugness, conventionality, respectability, and love of money." Galsworthy's "Island

Pharisees" and WAFT have much in common.   LJ is EMF's
worst novel.   Galsworthy's method of attack and EMF's are
the same.

458.   Gerber, Helmut E.   "Bibliographies, News, and Notes:
        E. M. Forster," English Fiction in Transition, IV, 1
        (1961), 20-22.

459.   Gerber, Helmut E. and Syed Hamid Husain.   "Bibli-
        ographies, News, and Notes: E. M. Forster," English
        Fiction in Transition, IV, 2 (1961), 45-53.

460.   Gerber, Helmut E.   "Bibliographies, News, and Notes:
        E. M. Forster," English Literature in Transition, IV,
        3 (1961), 41-47.

461.   Hoffman, Frederick J.   "Howards End and the Bogey
        of Progress," Modern Fiction Studies, VII (Autumn 1961),
        243-257.
            EMF saw history as "a ceaseless linear motion."
He sees "absolutes" as "evils" because they force the human
being into "acts of melodramatic self-vindication, and are
otherwise destructive of human balances."   This is one of the
reasons why HE is "so uncertain of progress."

462.   "Invalids," Times (London), (11 April 1961), 10, col. 6.
            A note to the effect that EMF, who had suffered a
heart attack Saturday [8 April], is "quite comfortable after a
satisfactory night."   He is in the hospital at Cambridge.

463.   Macdonald, Alastair A.   "Class-Consciousness in E.
        M. Forster," University of Kansas Review, XXVII
        (Spring 1961), 235-240.
            Class consciousness pervades EMF's novels.   He is
concerned with "the human predicament" and presents this
concern through persons and values of southern English, upper-
middle-class society.   It is a strength that he has done so because he has chosen material familiar to him.   It is also,
however, a weakness because issues upon which he builds the
more positive side of his work arise from "class-conditioned
attitudes."

464.   McDowell, Frederick P. W.   "Forster's 'Natural Super-
        naturalism': the Tales," Modern Fiction Studies, VII
        (Autumn 1961), 271-283.
            EMF's stories have not been extensively discussed.
"Mr. Andrews," "Co-ordination," and "The Curate's Friend"

fail to dramatize conclusively EMF's "complex and original concepts." "The Celestial Omnibus," "The Other Side of the Hedge" are "too arbitrarily conceived to become richly textured works." "Other Kingdom" and "The Story of a Panic" are "more authentic weldings of the realistic and the supernatural." In "Road from Colonus," "The Eternal Moment," "The Story of the Siren," "The Point of It," EMF has "more successfully ... combined the realistic with the fantastic, in order to achieve an increased degree of assent from the latter."

465.   Mulik, B. R. E. M. Forster's A Passage to India, (Critical Studies XXIV), Delhi: S. Chand and Co., 1961.
    A "review book" covering such topics as the "place of the novel in E. M. Forster's works"; its "Theme," i.e. "is it possible to be friendly with an Englishman"; PI as a "symbolical novel," and a "general estimate of the work."

465A.   O'Faolain, Sean. The Short Story: A Study in Pleasure. Boston: Little Brown, 1961. Index. pp. 441-444.
    A reprint of "The Story of the Siren" with an analysis.

466.   "Passage to India," Booklist, LVII (15 June 1961), 631.
    A review of the Rau dramatization. The play "lacks the novel's subtleties ... of character."

467.   "Passage to India," Bookmark, XX (April 1961), 104.
    A review of the Rau dramatization. "Fascinating."

468.   Rau, Santha Rama. A Passage to India: A Play from the Novel by E. M. Forster. New York: Harcourt, Brace and World, 1961. Also reprinted in Theatre Arts, XLVI (April 1962).

469.   Rolph, C. H., ed. The Trial of Lady Chatterley: Regina v. Penguin Books Ltd. Baltimore: Penguin Books, 1961. pp. 112-113.
    Gives EMF's testimony at the trial and notes, among other things, that he most admires Sons and Lovers.

470.   Sampson, George. The Concise Cambridge History of English Literature. Cambridge (Eng): University Press, 1961. Index. pp. 916, 962, 981-982, 994, 997, 1014, 1017.
    EMF's novels do not appear "dated" in the least, partly because of the "surprising strength of the humanist tradition" and partly because of his "preoccupation with those problems of morality and personal relationships which are not of an age

but for all time. "

471. Schorer, Mark. Modern British Fiction. New York:
     Oxford, 1961. pp. 195-209, 210-224.
          A reprint of "The Longest Journey and the Perils of
     Humanism, " by Frederick C. Crews (see: #416) and "The Twi-
     light of the Double Vision, " by Reuben Brower (see: #254).

472. Schorer, Mark. Sinclair Lewis, An American Life.
     New York: McGraw-Hill, 1961. Index. pp. 274, 311,
     516, 545-546.
          Lewis had almost no esteem for EMF. Neverthe-
     less, EMF was only one of the two British authors who con-
     gratulated him on winning the Nobel Prize.

473. Shusterman, David. "The Curious Case of Professor
     Godbole: A Passage to India Re-examined, " Publications
     of the Modern Language Association, LXXVI (Sept 1961),
     pp. 426-435.
          There is a grave mis-reading of the novel on the part
     of those who would turn EMF into a transplanted Hindu and
     his novel into little more than a tract for the glorification of
     Hinduism and of Godbole. It must be stressed that EMF never
     advocates complete detachment from human reality and from
     the world.

474. Sunday Times (London). Great Books of Our Times.
     London: Sunday Times, 1961. pp. 21, 33-34.
          Lists HE and notes that "the whole book is instinct
     with a wise humanity and a sense of posed social comedy, "
     however, PI is EMF's "greatest work. " It is the "humanist
     complement" to the "imaginative embodiment of the Raj in
     Kim. "

475. Thomson, George H. "Symbolism in E. M. Forster's
     Earlier Fiction, " Criticism, III (1961), 304-320.
          EMF's short stories are "early proof that [he] was
     fascinated by mythic purpose. "

476. Thomson, George H. "Theme and Symbol in Howards
     End. " Modern Fiction Studies, VII (Autumn 1961), 229-
     242. Reprinted in Shahane, V. A., ed. Perspectives
     on A Passage to India. New York: Barnes and Noble,
     1968.
          This attempt to define the meaning of the symbols in
     HE and to examine their connection with the theme is under-
     taken in the belief that the symbols are more precise in

meaning than has usually been thought.

477. Thomson, George H. "Thematic Symbol in A Passage
      to India, " Twentieth Century Literature, VII (July 1961),
      51-63.
         PI, like The Waste Land, is a study of twentieth
century man's spiritual condition. To develop its theme, EMF
employs "powerfully ordered symbols that are outwardly in
keeping with the realistic narrative and inwardly charged with
suggestion and meaning. "

478. Wilde, Alan. "The Aesthetic View of Life: Where
      Angels Fear to Tread, " Modern Fiction Studies, VII
      (Autumn 1961), 207-216.
         WAFT is ideal for studying EMF's technique and in-
tention because of its short length and relative simplicity of
plot. The latter proceeds melodramatically, which is a form
congenial to EMF's world-view. Its melodrama is "cousin to
the fantasy in his early stories. " It suggests a "theatrical
metaphor" which is appropriate to the book as a whole.

                            1962

479. Beach, Joseph Warren. English Literature of the 19th
      and Early 20th Centuries. Index. p. 246.
         EMF is a prime exponent of the psychological novel.

480. Beer, J. B. The Achievement of E. M. Forster.
      London: Chatto and Windus, 1962.
         I.   Aspects of a Novelist. Critics diverge in their
views of EMF. This stems from a basic uncertainty as to
how his novels ought to be read. It is not enough to read him
for his stories alone, nor for his social comedy alone, as
Rose Macaulay suggests. A more promising line is taken by
those who look at his work against the moral tradition of the
English novel. But there are drawbacks to a strictly moral
approach to his works. To understand EMF fully, one has
to see him as the spiritual heir of Blake, Coleridge, Shelley,
Beethoven, Wagner. While he admired Austen, those who
read him in a frame of mind that they associate with Austen
are due for a shock. Another side of EMF also presents a
difficulty: his combination of comedy and moral seriousness
with a strong admixture of emotion and imagination. The
difficulties he presents as a moralist are second only to those
he presents as a satirist. His morality is more likely to
guide his characters towards passion than to lead them away

from it. His imagination involves itself in his novels by giving
rise to symbolic patterns within the work as a whole. As a
result of his imagination and moral background EMF finds
himself confronted by the puzzling relationship between the inward imagination and the outer world of sense-perception.

          II. The Earth and the Stars. A summary of EMF's
life, his principal interests and their reflection in his art.

          III. From a View to Death. At first RWV seems a
straightforward social comedy when compared with EMF's
short stories. The main theme is familiar and presents no
difficulty. George is the protagonist of life, Cecil of art,
and Miss Bartlett of anti-life. For EMF, love is a state in
which the demands of head and heart are satisfied emotional-
ly. The various themes are given play by the leitmotifs he
uses. Music and art serve as underthemes to express the
forces which prevent Lucy from accepting Cecil's world and
drive her into George's. The central, "ministering theme,"
is one of "views and rooms." WAFT may be regarded as a
companion piece to RWV. In WAFT, Sawston is dismally representative of all London suburbs. It is drawn up in battle
array against Italy. In its opening chapters, EMF makes full
use of his gifts for domestic comedy. There is a "moral
struggle" between Sawston and Italy. The struggle centers
upon a society, Sawston, which thinks that people can be
treated as objects, and another, Italy, which makes many
mistakes but not that one. As a straightforward narrative,
the novel is a brilliant success in pitting Italian life against
Sawston's without understanding either the crudity and mess of
the one, or the "hooded wisdom" of the other. In this novel,
EMF has made his basic philosophy "esoteric" and dependent
upon one or two key passages. The relationship between
Caroline and Gino is the central fact which condemns every
other fact in the novel to varying degrees of unreality.

          IV. Flame Boats on a Stream. LJ marks a turning
point in EMF's development and is his most intensive achievement. The plot is essentially clear. EMF uses it to make
two points: one moral, the other psychological. It is a mis-
take to divide the characters into "sheep and goats." The
personal relationship between Rickie and his creator sometimes
operates with peculiar force. It is present in Rickie's occu-
pation with the stars. The central "visionary moment" in the
novel occurs in Chapter 33 when Stephen shows Rickie a
trick. The passage is one of EMF's "triumphs."

          V. In Country Sleep. HE complements the earlier
novel. Its over-all symbol is set firmly in space. The house
dominates the opening and the closing and is a presence
throughout. It is the main link between a realistic plot and a

pattern of symbolism which illuminates the world in general.
Not the least of the book's virtues is that it captures as a
running theme a feeling for the house. This is rare in
English literature. The book, however, "just misses great-
ness." EMF fails with Leonard Bast, but the failure supplies the point of development for his next novel.
        VI. The Undying Worm. The seeds of PI were grow-
ing in LJ. There is an "inevitability" in EMF's choice of
theme in the novel. In the earlier novels, Sawston never quite
found an antagonist worthy of its powers. In India, it did in
a separate civilization which was more comprehensive, more
venerable, more alive to the human condition than itself. The
dramatic situation in PI is finely conceived. Nevertheless,
the plot is a disappointment to some. Its structure does not
consist merely of an arrangement of events. A common interpretation of the work is that it is a polemic against the
British rule in India. It is, in reality, "an exploration of
extremes." There are several patterns in the novel. Symbolic implications broaden these patterns from a conflict between the British and the Indians to that between earth and
sky, spirit and matter, love and the intractable. Everything
in PI must be confronted by the Marabar caves; they are a
"touchstone" by means of which reality is tested.
        VII. Serving the World. In style and subject mat-
ter, PI is a considerable advance on the previous novels.
This is due in part to WWI. EMF's chief memorial of his
non-combative experience in that war is Alex and PP. Through
the 20's and 30's his literary position remained firm but un-
obtrusive. His distinctive contribution lies in his exploration
of what happens when body and imagination are both active in
love and of the relation between this "glorious effect and the
sense of reality."
        VIII. In and Out of Time. EMF could not have writ-
ten a new novel without a "firm and difficult departure from
all that had gone before," because PI presents themes which
formulate a "complete universe." Many of the peculiarities
of his writing spring from his desire to work between domestic
comedy and a "romantic intensity of vision." His usual habit
is to suggest by understatement. His moral stands can only
be stated properly in terms of his basic philosophy, which is
that if humans do not succeed in being true to head and heart,
they cannot live in a real world.

481. Bradbury, Malcolm. "E. M. Forster's Howards End,"
      Critical Quarterly, IV (Autumn 1962), 229-241. Revised
      as "Howards End" in his Forster: a Collection of Critical
      Essays.   Englewood Cliffs, New Jersey: Prentice-Hall,
      1966.

HE is a novel treated in the comic mode about the circumstances in which the moral life can be led in society, about the compromises it must effect within itself if it is to do so, and the moral necessity for making such compromises. A critical irony dominates the book.

482. Brander, Laurence. "E. M. Forster and India," Review of English Literature, III (Oct 1962), 76-84. Discusses the various Indian elements found in PI.

483. Churchill, Thomas. "Place and Personality in Howards End," Critique, V (Spring-Summer 1962), 61-73. In HE, EMF seems to have symbolized an ordered possibility that individuals might "connect," a "kind of hope existing, if not in 'life,' in soil, landscape, and place, and in the tradition that these entities imply." Moving chapter by chapter through the novel, Brander shows that although EMF's "dialectical views may have insisted that people of different ranks, intellects, and of sensibilities must try to connect ... his artistic conscience forbade these connections."

484. "Comic Moralist," Times (London), (2 Aug 1962), 13, col. 3. A review of J. B. Beer's The Achievement of E. M. Forster. Beer notes that EMF is a "restless writer." There is a "tension" in his work between detachment and passion, skepticism and mysticism, the belief in cool reason and the sense of natural magic. Beer's book is useful and readable.

485. Crews, Frederick C. E. M. Forster: The Perils of Humanism. Princeton: Princeton University Press, 1962. I. Introductory. EMF is an Edwardian in point of time and in spirit. The modern revolutions in psychology, physics, politics, even in literary style, while they have not escaped him, have not influenced him. II. Forster and Religion: From Clapham to Bloomsbury. It is impossible to neglect the importance of religious questions in EMF's novels. His anti-clericalism and his light regard for Christian theology can, however, give a one-sided view of his religious position. He is an agnostic complicated by romantic evasions. He has a thwarted fascination with the Absolute. III. The Refuge of Liberalism. The relevance of his political views to his novels is not obvious. In a refined sense it is possible to see political meaning in his novels.

Their lack of overt partisanship follows consistently with his version of liberalism. His non-fiction leaves no doubt as to the central position occupied by his political beliefs in his moral framework.

IV. <u>Cambridge and "the Good."</u> For EMF there are certain values that might be called "absolute goods." Sincerity, art, private personal relationships, and his feeling for the English countryside and its tradition are some.

V. <u>The Longest Journey.</u> The problem in the novel --the position of having to reconcile the world of Cambridge with the demands of ordinary existence--is not one simply of "adjustment." His question is whether the purposeful, individualistic pursuit of the Good and the Beautiful has a right to exist at all. As a philosophical novel, LJ undertakes to cope with such questions as what is a man's relationship to his own past, his future; where should he place his faith, etc.

VI. <u>The Italian Novels.</u> WAFT and RWV are similar in tone, theme, and setting. EMF's mode is that of social comedy. The moral issue is the familiar one of whether we should heed the voice of passion or of respectability. He believes in passion but is also aware of its dangers. These are highly polished books.

VII. <u>The Comic Spirit.</u> EMF's preoccupation as an artist has been with finding a viable symbolism. Comedy supplies the counterweight which keeps the symbolism from slipping too far toward allegory.

VIII. <u>Howards End.</u> The novel puts into dramatic terms the creed of liberalism. Its framework is a series of antitheses between liberalism and its opposite. The plot involves an extended test of liberalism's ability to come to grips and to terms with its adversary. It is the one novel in which EMF projects a reasonable hope for the survival of liberalism.

IX. <u>The Limitations of Mythology.</u> With HE, the stages of EMF's career began to assume an intelligible order. His art acquires a new seriousness of purpose, intricacy of plot and symbolism, and a broadening of social and metaphysical references. It becomes possible to recognize an extension of the total meaning of his fictional universe. This can be seen with his handling of technical devices: the gradual disappearance of allusions to mythology. His use of myth is "Apollonian" but his early stories show a distinct hospitality to the idea of Dionysianism. Of all of his novels, LJ is most deeply imbued with myth and it is the one whose meaning depends most crucially upon the interpretation of its myth.

X. <u>A Passage to India.</u> PI is EMF's best but most difficult novel to interpret. Trilling comes closest in his

interpretation.   The book is unified by the principle that unity
is not obtainable.   The plot is trivial.
         XI.   The Importance of Reason.   His eclecticism is
the one element which distinguishes EMF from most liberals
and is the most important element in his sensibility.   No
faith stands up well in his novels, not even humanism.   AH
and Two and each of his novels get their structure from this
eclecticism.   PI is the "culminating expression of his refinement of liberalism."   While anchored to it, PI is aware of the
weaknesses of the liberal tradition.   EMF's "nearly suicidal
eclecticism" becomes a "weapon for aesthetic victory over the
partiality and error it reveals."   The victory belongs to reason, but "to reason defining the limits of reason."

486.   Echeruo, M. J. C.   "E. M. Forster and the 'Unde-
         veloped Heart, ' " English Studies in Africa, V (September
         1962), 151-155.
         EMF seems to suggest in his novels that the "dis-
satisfactions of love, difficulties in personal relationships,
and the pursuit of the wrong values in life are all the product
of the 'undeveloped heart, ' " i. e. of a person who has not been
allowed to develop his "natural lines."   This atrophy of heart
is caused by money and social standing.

487.   Entwhistle, William J. and Eric Gillett.   The Literature
         of England, A.D. 500-1960: A Survey of British Litera-
         ture from the Beginnings to the Present Day.   London:
         London: Longmans, 1962.   Index. pp. 209, 215, 246.
         Joyce, Woolf, Aldous Huxley and EMF are the four
novelists who have exercised the greatest influence upon and
have evoked the loudest plaudits from their younger contemporaries and from intellectual circles on both sides of the
Atlantic.   EMF writes precisely.   He is a conscious and fas-
tidious writer whose creative impulse is not very strong.

488.   Forster, Edward Morgen.   "Indian Entries from a
         Diary, " with an introduction by Santha Rama Rau.
         Harper's Magazine, CCXXIV (Feb 1962), 46-52.
         (An annotation of Rau's introduction only).   One can
trace many of the real people and actual incidents which were
included in PI in EMF's jottings.   In Syed Ross Masood can
be traced the character of Aziz, and the landscape of the
Marabar Caves can be found in the countryside of Chhatapur.
In this diary is the "raw material of a great novel."

489.   Gerber, Helmut E. , Edward S. Lauterbach, Edwin
         Nierenberg, Syed Hamid Hussain.   "Bibliography, News

and Notes: E. M. Forster," <u>English Fiction in Transition,</u>
V, 1 (1962), 38-43.

490. Gerber, Helmut E., Edward S. Lauterbach, Syed Hamid
Hussain, Helga S. Gerber, and James G. Kennedy.
"Bibliography, News, and Notes: E. M. Forster,"
<u>English Fiction in Transition,</u> V, 4 (1962), 25-32.

491. Hannah, Donald. "The Limitations of Liberalism in
E. M. Forster's Works," <u>English Miscellany: A Symposium of History, Literature and the Arts,</u> XIII (1962),
165-178.
 EMF's work poses a problem. Is his personality as
a novelist so dominant in his novels that it really dwarfs
them? If so, then the books are read as "attributes of the
public figure" and not in their own right. There is a possibility that certain "qualities" and "values" believed to be expressed by the novels "are simply not there."

492. Hollingsworth, Keith, "A Passage to India: The Echoes
in the Marabar Caves," <u>Criticism, IV (Summer 1962),</u>
210-224. Reprinted in <u>Shahane, V. A., ed. Perspectives on E. M. Forster's A Passage to India, A Collection
of Critical Essays.</u> New York: Barnes and Noble, 1968.
 Every effort to explain the echoes reduces and flattens
them because they are genuine symbols. This is the case
with the explanation offered in this article. The echo suggests
a mockery of communication; on a lower level, it suggests the
delusion of Western culture. The echo belongs essentially to
Mrs. Moore, who represents Christianity, and to Adela, rep-
resenting English rationalism, both of whom are revealed as
deluded.

493. Karl, Frederick. <u>The Contemporary English Novel.</u>
New York: Farrar, Straus and Cudahy, 1962. Index.
pp. 6, 11, 18, 86, 109, 111, 195, 272.
 Notes that P. H. Newby combines the social ideas
of EMF and Waugh's sense of confusion in <u>The Picnic at
Sakkara.</u> Henry Green's <u>Rock (Concluding)</u> resembles Mr.
Emerson. EMF has helped to put the notion of "hero" into
an early grave.

494. Kermode, Frank. "The One Orderly Product (E. M.
Forster)," in <u>Puzzles and Epiphanies: Essays and Reviews, 1958-1961.</u> London: Routledge and Kegan Paul,
1962.
 EMF is a "kind of symbolist." PI, like any novel,

"fakes human relationships but also, working against muddle
and chance, fakes an idea of order, without which those relationships have no significance."

495. Lawrence, A. W., ed. Letters to T. E. Lawrence.
     London: Jonathan Cape, 1962. Index. pp. 58-75.
        A series of letters from EMF to TEL. EMF calls
him a "granular" writer as opposed to the "fluid" type.
Praises Seven Pillars of Wisdom and calls it a "poem."
Agrees with TEL's concept of The Plumed Serpent which TEL
reviewed anonymously in Spectator, 6 Aug 1927. Calls TEL's
The Mint good. It proves, he continues, that TEL can "write
creatively about anything that happens [to him]."

496. Lehmann, John. "E. M. Forster: A Refusal to be
     Great?" London Magazine, NS. II (7 Oct 1962), 74-78.
        A review of Gransden's E. M. Forster and Beer's
The Achievement of E. M. Forster. Both volumes are
good and can be usefully read together. They both make it
clear that the two basic reasons for EMF's power of survival
are first, his extreme subtlety of craftsmanship, and second,
the depth of his convictions as a poet-philosopher.

497. "Lives and Works," Times (London), (12 April 1962),
     19, col. 5.
        A review of Gransden's E. M. Forster. The volume
is "clear, uncomplicated and persuasive" but "we miss something of his [EMF's] charm and unpredictability." Nevertheless the book is "careful and attractive."

498. McDowell, Frederick P. W. "The Newest Elucidations
     of Forster," English Fiction in Transition, V. 4 (1962),
     51-58.
        Reviews criticism of EMF by McConkey (The Novels
of E. M. Forster), Oliver (The Art of E. M. Forster). He
notes that the latter is the slightest in substance of recent
studies.

499. Millgate, Michael. "Scott Fitzgerald as Social Novel-
     ist: Statement and Technique in 'The Great Gatsby,' "
     Modern Language Review, LVII (1962), 335-339.
        What is striking is how alike EMF and Fitzgerald
are in their imagery, use of symbols, their rhetorical gift,
and feeling for their native lands.

500. Moseley, Edwin M. "Christ as One Avatar: Forster's
     A Passage to India," in Pseudonyms of Christ in the

Modern Novel: Motifs and Methods. Pittsburgh: University of Pittsburgh Press, 1962. pp. 153-162.

Other than Faulkner, EMF is the only modern writer who has a "relativistic and anthropological approach." PI is a novel which makes "a universal point through the conscious employment of multi-cultural rituals and meanings."

501. Moseley, Edwin M. "A New Correlative for Howards End: Demeter and Persephone," Lock Haven Bulletin (State Teachers College, Lock Haven, Pa.), Ser. #3 (1962).

In ways "clear and subtle, positive and ironic, in almost too many ways to restate," the narrative of EMF's HE has as its chief correlative the myth of Demeter and Persephone.

502. "Passage to India," Library Journal, LXXXVII (15 Jan 1962), 346.

A review of the Rau dramatization. The author has succeeded in capturing the essence of the book. It is "a moving drama in its own right."

503. "A Passage to India on Broadway," Times (London), (2 Feb 1962), 13, col. 4.

A review of the Rau dramatization, New York, 1 Feb. A note to the effect that the London production of Rau's Passage to India won the approval of Broadway drama critics, although some found the story "puzzling." Taubman of the New York Times found it "arresting and timely," Chapman of the Daily News "confessed puzzlement at the slender but gracefully told story."

504. Rodrigues, E. L. "Towards an Understanding of E. M. Forster," Journal of the Maharaja Sayajirao University of Baroda, XI (April 1962), 91-105.

A general review of EMF's work and philosophy.

505. "Search for Connection," Times Literary Supplement (London), (22 June 1962), 460.

A review of Beer's The Achievement of E. M. Forster and Gransden's E. M. Forster. Because EMF has hungered after "essence," he is sometimes uneasily ambivalent. Both authors have written very useful and illuminating commentaries. But they might have made more use of what there is available about EMF the man instead of once again going over what is already well known and documented.

506. Taubman, Howard. "Theatre: Timely Theme, "Passage to India" Bows at the Ambassador," New York Times, (1 Feb 1962), 23, col. 1.
        A review of the Rau dramatization. Though the novel was published in the 20's, its theme remains "vitally permanent." It is impossible to sit through this "clever dramatization" without being aware of its "timelessness."

507. Taubman, Howard. "Worth Adapting: Much of Quality of Forster Novel in Santha Rama Rau's Play," New York Times, (11 Feb 1962), Sect. II, 1, col. 1.
        In view of the novel's "complexity of texture and subtlety of sensibility," it is "astonishing how much of its atmosphere, emotion, and thought have been carried over to the stage."

508. "Theatrical Notes," New York Times, (2 May 1962), 31, col. 1.
        Notes that the Rau dramatization of PI, starring Eric Portman and Gladys Cooper, will give its 110th and final performance, Saturday, 5 May, at the Ambassador Theater.

509. Tuohy, Frank. "The English Question," Spectator, CCVIII (6 July 1962), 30-31.
        A review of Beer's The Achievement of E. M. Forster. The book may well intimidate those of EMF's admirers who can keep turning to him without feeling any necessity to "pin him down." Beer "emphasizes" the romantic, visionary element in the novels in a way which has not been done before."

510. Watson, George. The Literary Critics; A Study of English Descriptive Criticism. London: Penguin Books, 1962. Index. p. 186.

511. Watts, Stephen. "Forster on 'India,' Author Talks About Novel-Into-Play," New York Times, (28 Jan 1962), Sect. II, 1, col. 3+.
        The novelist had never thought of the work as a play until Miss Rau came up with the idea. There was, however, a radio version of the book by Lance Sieveking several years before which "impressed" him. He did not think that the Rau play would be a commercial success.

512. Weimer, Sanford R. and David H. Stewart. "Forster's A Passage to India," Explicator, XX (May 1962), item #73.

Modes of transportation have two functions in PI; they reveal and define characters in terms of class or caste and they assist in the action.

1963

513. "The Arts: Forster Issues Simplified; Drastic Effect of Adaptation; Arts Theatre: Where Angels Fear to Tread," Times (London), (7 June 1963), 15, Col. 1.
    Elizabeth Hart made a "neat, old-fashioned play out of Where Angels Fear to Tread." It "coarsens the original" and "what does come as a surprise is its triviality." The sense of moral ambiguity has "largely evaporated." The characters "cannot develop" and the play simplifies the issues so much that it becomes a "period piece."

514. "The Arts: Graceful Play from Novel, Forster Skill-fully Adapted; St. Martin's Theatre: Where Angels Fear to Tread," Times (London), (10 July 1963), 13, col. 1.
    The play is "good theatre," though a little slow but consistent in its stylization of speech and manner. "Admir-ers of Mr. Forster might, of course, expect more." The actors: Dulcie Gray, Michael Dennison, Violet Farebrother. Directed by Glenn Byam Shaw and adapted by Elizabeth Hart.

515. Cooperman, Stanley. "The Imperial Posture and the Shrine of Darkness: Kipling's Naulahka and E. M. Forster's A Passage to India." English Literature in Transition, VI, 1 (1963), 9-13.
    Kipling's novel uses "almost precisely the same crisis in plot mechanism as the ... Marabar Caves episode." For Kipling, the "Cow's Mouth" provides "a major point of negation no less explicit than do EMF's caves."

516. Cox, C. B. The Free Spirit: A Study of Liberal Humanism in the Novels of George Eliot, Henry James, E. M. Forster, Virginia Woolf, and Angus Wilson. London: Oxford University Press, 1963. pp. 74-102.
    EMF stands for the liberal tradition proclaiming the values of freedom, progress, and intelligence. His comic art is a continuous exploration of the flaws which appear when those ideals are put into practice. He is a moral realist. His value for the liberal imagination is that, for him, life is made up of "muddle."

517. Dobrée, Bonamy. The Lamp and the Lute: Studies in Six Modern Authors. New York: Russell & Russell,

1963. pp. 66-85.
EMF is among the first of the "new novelists" who "use their works to explore life." With his very first work, there is a feeling that here "is somebody with an interesting and original mind working out a problem" important to himself and to us. It is expressed and worked out in terms of art.

518. Eapen, Karippacheril Chakko. "E. M. Forster and India," Dissertation Abstracts, XXIII (1963), 3897.
EMF's "kinship" with Hinduism is clearly reflected in the Hindu symbolism and theology which he uses in PI to give the novel "depth and meaning."

519. Griffin, Lloyd. "E. M. Forster: A Tribute, Edited by Natwar-Singh and Others" (review), Library Journal, LXXXVIII (15 Dec 1963), 4761.
EMF is revealed as a "curious and paradoxical blend of sensitivity, humility, and over-civilized sophistication." The volume is "not a definitive critique but a pleasant and informative book."

520. Hart, Elizabeth Dillingham. Where Angels Fear to Tread, A Play in Two Acts. Italian dialogue by Gita Denise. London: S. French, 1963.

521. Husain, Syed Hamid. "E. M. Forster," English Literature in Transition, VI, 3 (1963), 161-162.
An annotated bibliography.

522. Kennedy, James G. "E. M. Forster," English Literature in Transition, VI, 1 (1963), 31-32.
An annotated bibliography.

523. Kennedy, James G. "E. M. Forster," English Literature in Transition, VI, 2 (1963), 97-105.
An annotated bibliography.

524. Kennedy, James G. "E. M. Forster," English Literature in Transition, VI, 4 (1963), 229-233.
An annotated bibliography.

525. Missey, James Lawrence. "Appearance and Reality in the Fiction of E. M. Forster," Dissertation Abstracts, XXIV (1963), 2037-38.
This study is a description of the theme of appearance and reality which exists in one of two forms or in both forms in all of EMF's novels, and in most of his short stories.

526. Muir, Edwin. The Structure of the Novel. London:
Hogarth Press, 1963.
Makes use of Aspects to illustrate his position on the
novel, most especially in Chapters I and IV.

527. Nierenberg, Edwin H. "Two Essays on Man: Alexander Pope and E. M. Forster," Dissertation Abstracts,
XXIII (1963), 4678.
Both authors were "prophet-like" in their exploration
of a complex universe that offers a basis for choice and value through eclecticism, the selection from among various possible ways of thought, of faith, and of reality.

528. Rueckert, William H. Kenneth Burke and the Drama of
Human Relations. Minneapolis: University of Minnesota
Press, 1963. Index. pp. 110-111, 179-190.
Discusses the "dialectical structure" of PI and
analyzes HE.

529. Shahane, V. A. "Symbolism in A Passage to India:
Temple," English Studies (Groninger, Holland), XLIV
(Dec 1963), 423-431. Reprinted in Shahane, V. A., ed.
Perspectives on E. M. Forster's A Passage to India.
New York: Barnes and Noble, 1968.
This article attempts to expound the significance of
the third section of PI in a new way and its main objective is
to disprove R. A. Brower's contention that "the Temple" is
"most crudely ironic." The symbol of the echo, he contends,
is more crude.

530. Sorenson, Philip E. "E. M. Forster: A Brief Memoir," Claremont Quarterly, XI (Autumn 1963), 5-9.
The author shared a "brief but happy" friendship
with EMF in the summer of 1961. The hours spent with
him were "seldom devoted to critical discussion."

531. Stewart, J. I. M. Eight Modern Writers. Oxford:
The Clarendon Press, 1963. Index. pp. 16, 32, 76,
111, 128, 245, 264, 465.
EMF disliked Ulysses and called it "an epic of grub-
biness and disillusion." He also noted that only "maimed
creatures can alone breathe" in the pages of Henry James.

532. Warner, Rex. "A Passage to India and Beyond," New
York Times Book Review, (29 Dec 1963), 1.
A review of Natwar-Singh's E. M. Forster: A
Tribute. These personal tributes are "all both moving and il-
luminating." They are also "revealing."

533. Wheeler, Robert Harvey. "Poetry, Comedy, and
      Vitalism in the Novels of E. M. Forster," Dissertation
      Abstracts, XXIV (1963), 2045.
         The dissertation endeavors to refute the argument
that EMF's practice of combining social comedy with a poetic
voice fails to coalesce, and that the poetry itself is indistinct
in its reference.

534. "Where Angels Fear to Tread is Staged in London,"
      Times (London), (8 June 1963), 14, col. 6.
         Notes that the adaptation by Elizabeth Hart is "faith-
ful to the spirit of the original" but "the lesson of love that
permeates the novel tends to get lost."

                              1964

535. Austin, Edgar A. "Rites of Passage in A Passage to
      India," Orient/West, IX (May-June 1964), 64-72.
         Though the plot of PI is built around Adela's "fright"
in the Marabar Caves, Mrs. Moore's experience appears to
hold the "meaning of the book."

536. Bedient, Calvin Bernard. "The Fate of the Self:
      Self and Society in the Novels of George Eliot, D. H.
      Lawrence and E. M. Forster," Dissertation Abstracts,
      XXV (1964), 1187.
         PI is "poised uncertainly between humanism and re-
ligion--between personality and Brahman West and East." In
HE an "ethic of reconciliation ... gives way to an ethic of
connection between the seen and the unseen, an ethic more
passive and less concerned with humanity, yet EMF's allegi-
ence continues to be with the individual."

537. Campbell, Sandy. "Mr. Forster of King's,"
      Mademoiselle, LIX (June 1964), 80-81.
         A record of the visit of the author to EMF's apart-
ment in King's College, Cambridge. EMF likes most of all
LJ. He also liked the London production of Rau's dramatization of PI. EMF gave up fiction because "the kind of
English family life [he] understood ... has disappeared."

538. "E. M. Forster: a Bibliography," Bulletin of Bibli-
      ography, XXIV (Sept 1964), 108-111.

539. Friedman, Albert B. "Forster, Dostoyevsky, Akuta-
      gawa, and 'St. Peter and His Mother,'" English
      Language Notes, I (June 1964), 286-291.

Traces the origin of the tales told to Alyosha by
Grushenka (The Brothers Karamazov, VII, iii, 7) about
which EMF wrote a paper for the literary society of the
Indian State of Dewas Senior, for whose Maharaja he was
secretary.

540. Gallagher, M. "Aspects of the Novel and Crews's
     E. M. Forster: The Perils of Humanism, " Studies,
     LIII (Summer 1964), 213.
     A review of the Penguin edition of Aspects and of
the Crews study. Talks in Aspects are "brilliantly penetrating at times" and give the "impression that common sense
is always in control." Crews avoids "the pitfall of the
Forster critic, " in that he "neither sneers at nor worships
the master and his work." He starts with the premise that
EMF is a "novelist of ideas." The central thesis is that
EMF's development involves the progressive "facing up" to
the insecurities and perils inherent in the liberal-humanist
tradition.

541. Garnett, David. "E. M. Forster and John Galsworthy, "
     Review of English Literature (Leeds), V (Jan 1964), 7-18.
     Both authors attacked British upper middle class
"philistine complacency from the inside." Both did their best
work at the same time. WAFT and The Island Pharisees
"turn on a disturbing foreigner showing up the inhumanity of
the British upperclass." The method of attack is the same
for both authors.

542. Hardy, Barbara. The Appropriate Form: An Essay
     on the Novel. London: University of London. Index.
     pp. 8, 9, 36, 51, 73-82, 121-123, 130, 136, 180, 207.
     EMF's novels are written as "ethical rather than
metaphysical arguments." They are "tentative and even
ambivalent in their answers." They do, however, provide
answers and these are answers to the "plainly imposed question of the significance of life." There then follow analyses
of the novels.

543. Hardy, John Edward. Man in the Modern Novel.
     Seattle: University of Washington Press, 1964. Index.
     pp. 33, 175, et passim.
     Notes EMF's attack on the Conradian "obscurity"
and his comments on Virginia Woolf are summarized.

544. Harrison, Gilbert A. "The Modern Mr. Forster, "
     New Republic, CL (11 Jan 1964), 15-16.

A record of a visit to EMF by the author. "Tolerance
at least, affection at best, is the message" of all of EMF's
books. He is "a moralist without Belief."

545. Harrison, Robert Ligon. "The Manuscript of A Passage
     to India," Dissertation Abstracts, XXV (1964), 474.
     The purpose is to present the student of EMF with
a "vision of the novel as a work in progress." A class jux-
tapositioning of variants is given.

546. Horowitz, Ellin. "The Communal Ritual and the Dying
     God in E. M. Forster's A Passage to India," Criticism,
     V (Winter 1964), 70-88.
     PI is "neither sociological nor mythical but socio-
anagogical; thus the very framework or attitude both implies
and resolves opposition."

547. Hynes, S. "Old Man at King's," Commonweal, LXXIX
     (21 Feb 1964), 635-638.
     Critics have treated EMF with "that affectionate
respect which one accords the very old [who] have outlived
their own era." His novels are "Edwardian" in terms not
only of their publication dates but in their "atmosphere and
in their values." His stories are "not distinguished, except
for one or two," but they do demonstrate certain of his "values and habits of mind--his Victorian Hellenism, his visionary romanticism, etc." His first two novels are "social come-
dies"; LJ is "the least successful" of his books; his last two,
HE and PI, are the "most serious, the most didactic, the
most symbolical, and ... most ambitious" of all of his
novels.

548. Joseph, David I. The Art of Rearrangement: E. M.
     Forster's Abinger Harvest. New Haven: Yale Universi-
     ty Press, 1964.
     The volume was originally an essay submitted in
partial fulfillment of the requirement for the English Honors
Program at Yale. AH suggests two possible approaches: it
can be understood independently as an anthology complete in
itself, or its essays can be employed separately to illuminate
specific themes and incidents within EMF's novels. Joseph
uses neither approach exclusively. The subject matter of
AH resembles closely the concerns of its author's novels.
Joseph attempts to demonstrate that the form in which AH is
cast represents a "genuine medium of expression" and that
the problems which EMF chose to examine in his novels are
re-examined in this work. A chapter is devoted to each of

AH's books.

549. Missey, James Lawrence. "Forster's Redemptive
      Siren, " Modern Fiction Studies, X (Winter 1964-1965),
      383-385.
          Trilling and McDowell have "so seriously misin-
terpreted "The Story of the Siren" that a correction seems
justified. Both see the siren as a symbol of evil or of death.
Missey maintains that it suggests "hope, love, and salvation. "

550. Natwar-Singh, K. E. M. Forster: A Tribute, with
      Selections from His Writings on India. New York: Har-
      court, Brace and World, 1964.
          The volume makes no claim to being a critical analy-
sis or reassessment of EMF's achievement as a writer. It
is divided into two parts. Part I includes personal recollec-
tions of EMF by Raja Rao, Ahmed Ali, Mulk Raj Anand,
Santha Rama Rau, and K. Natwar-Singh. Part II includes
selections from EMF's writings on India: "Mahatma Ghandi, "
"The Nine Gems of Ujjain, " "Syed Ross Masood, " "On the
Death of Bapu Sahib, " "Note on A Passage to India, " "Caves, "
"India Again, " "The Mind of the Indian State, " "Gokul Ashtami, "
"Hymn Before Action. "

551. Nierenberg, Edwin. "The Prophecy of E. M. Forster, "
      Queen's Quarterly, LXXI (Spring 1964), 189-202.
          EMF is a "prophet of reformation. " He is a "re-
minder that the spiritual life is necessary, mysterious, and
real. " Though he criticizes the traditional religious concepts
and terms of Christianity, he uses them nevertheless. He
would agree with Alexander Pope that the end of religion is
the establishment of the universal brotherhood of man through
love.

552. Nierenberg, Edwin. "The Withered Priestess: Mrs.
      Moore's Incomplete Passage to India, " Modern Language
      Association Quarterly, XXV (June 1964), 198-204. Re-
      printed in Shahane, V. A. Perspectives on E. M.
      Forster's A Passage to India. New York: Barnes and
      Noble, 1968.
          Mrs. Moore, if not a failure, is certainly not a
heroine even though much of the criticism of PI stresses her
"benevolent and even superhuman qualities. " She is "neither
a saint nor a devil, neither an altogether redemptive nor yet
a fallen character, " but "one with concurrent attributes of
sincerity and self-deception, of true and false virtues. "

553. Nordell, Roderick.   "He Uplifted and Enlarged Our
      Lives," Christian Science Monitor, (2 Jan 1964), 7.
        A review of Natwar-Singh's E. M. Forster: A Trib-
ute.   On his 85th birthday, EMF's name "still has an aura
unlike that surrounding any other living novelist." No critical
comments on the book are given.

554. Prescott, Orville.   "Mr. Forster and His Indian
      Friends," New York Times, (1 Jan 1964), 23, col. 5.
        A review of Natwar-Singh's E. M. Forster: A Trib-
ute.   The tributes are not concerned so much with his body of
work but with some of his ideas and even more with his personality.   His friends regard him as "a great writer ... a
seer, poet, prophet and saint." The essays vary in quality.
The least successful is by Raja Rao and the best by Santha
Rama Rau.

555. Reed, John R.   Old School Ties: The Public Schools in
      British Literature. Syracuse (New York): Syracuse Uni-
      versity Press, 1964.   Index.
        On spontaneity of feelings, 125, 142, 143; bourgeois
values in writings of, 125-126, 137; view of English character, 126; on reality, 126-127, 130-131, 132, 139, 143, 150-
151, 153, 307n.; public school product in writings of, 127-
128, 146-148, 152-153, 259; on love, 131, 140-141, 144, 153,
307n.; on muddleheadedness, 136, 139-140, 151; criticism of
public schools, 137, 143-144, 259, 305n.; criticism of
Empire literary material for, 145; on public school religion,
148; HE, 137-142; LJ, 126-136, 305n, 307n; PI, 146-154,
307n; RWV, 143.

556. Saunders, J. W.   The Profession of English Letters.
      London: Routledge and Kegan Paul, 1964. Index. pp.
      223-224, 243.
        EMF's views of life is "unique." No other writer
"quite captures with the same skill the power of the chance
collisions of human beings" and the "intangibility of all human
relationships."

557. Walsh, William.   A Human Idiom: Literature and Hu-
      manity. London: Chatto and Windus, 1964. Index. p.
      119.
        Quotes F. R. Leavis's remarks on EMF.

558. Waugh, Evelyn.   A Little Learning. Boston: Little,
      Brown, 1964. Index. pp. 37, 198-199.
        One of Waugh's favorite books was PP.

559. Westbury, Barry R. "Forster's 5th Symphony: Another
      Aspect of Howards End, " Modern Fiction Studies, X
      (Winter 1964-1965), 359-365.
          EMF makes a "great deal out of" Helen's reaction to
      Beethoven's 5th Symphony. This reaction symbolizes "the
      overall movement in HE towards synthesis of opposites into
      a steady and whole vision of life. Her "synathesia" is used
      to reflect the highly desirable experience of synthesis, of
      unity of being.

560. Wilde, Alan. Art and Order, A Study of E. M.
      Forster. New York: New York University Press, 1964.
          I. Art and Life: Biographical and Introductory.
      EMF's world can be understood to be chiefly concerned with
      art and order, although they are not the only concerns of his
      books. They are important to understand if his world is to be
      understood. This work sets out to trace them and to "present
      an angle of vision" from which the world can be observed.
          II. The Aesthetic View of Life. 1. WAFT--His
      first novel is ideal for studying EMF's technique and intention.
      Melodrama serves as a "structural counterpart" to what may
      be called his "philosophy of the great moment. " The opposi-
      tion between Italy and England provides the backdrop for the
      action. 2. LJ--In it, he fails to achieve sufficient distance
      from the problems that most interest him to use them proper-
      ly. It fails in "coherence and integralness. " Too much is
      attempted; too little accomplished. Nevertheless, it carries
      on many of the concerns of WAFT. 3. RWV--In many ways
      this is his "best-controlled and most perfectly realized"
      novel. It is slighter, however, in scale and intention than
      some of the other books. Yet, it succeeds in doing almost
      everything it sets out to do. It is, in a sense, "a coda" to
      the novels which precede it. Its concerns are similar, but
      its manner is different. The major theme is expressed in
      the contrast between two opposed responses to life. It op-
      erates by an opposition, constantly repeated, of one set of
      values against another.
          III. Two Worlds and Their Ways: The Short Stories.
      They are less ambitious than the novels. What makes most
      of them "minor works of art" is their "conceptions" rather
      than their lengths. They are more overtly fabulous and
      moral since they are based upon the opposition between the
      forces of good and evil, unrelieved by subtle investigations
      into the psychologies of the characters. They are valuable
      as guides to EMF's preoccupations and the changes in mood
      and direction of his work.
          IV. The Search for Order. 1. HE. It is EMF's

most ambitious attempt to complete successfully his search
for order and harmony. " This attempt, however, is "under-
mined throughout the book by his own doubts and hesitancies. "
There is a more fundamental ambivalence between hope and
despair than in any other of his books. It is the plot that
works most obviously in a general way toward the reconciliation of opposed ideas and characters. Helen Schlegel is a
more dramatic, less complex woman than her sister Margaret. Margaret's character is relatively predictable. The
other characters are "no more satisfactory than Margaret. "
2. PI--There is a gulf which separates this novel from the
others. It presents "the final resolution of the various attempts at a consistent attitude toward the world expressed in
the earlier works. " From this vantage, the work appears to
be the culmination of a steady development. Nevertheless, it
differs in kind and in degree from the others. The early
pages of Pt. I involve an illustration of the relations between
the British and the Indians. Pt. II is given over to "the expression of ... anarchic primitivism" and to an "indication of
the effects on the characters of the vision it inspires. " Pt.
III describes the festival celebrating the birth of the god
Krishna. The chapter which discusses the festival serves to
introduce the themes and symbols which are to be developed
and is itself the "most important and colorful scene" in Pt.
III. The final message of the section is "not a total affirmation of Hinduism, but the recognition that man must have some
relation with the unexplained and the unexplainable. "
       V. Art and Order. Though EMF produced no novels
after PI, his concern with the problems of order continued in
his nonfictional writing in which the problem was at least resolved by an affirmation of art.

561. Woolf, Leonard Sidney. Beginning Again: An Autobi-
       ography of the Years 1911-1918. London: Hogarth Press,
       1964. Index. pp. 22-24.
       Speaks of EMF's early connection with the Bloomsbury
group and its "inoculation" with "Moore and Moorism. "

                              1965

562. Allen, Walter. The Modern Novel in Britain and the
       United States. New York: Dutton, 1965. Index. pp.
       33-34, 39, 110, 185, 247.
       Aspects, 27; his technique old-fashioned, 36; a
tragic humanist, 36-37; PI, 37-38; Christopher Isherwood on,
237.

563. "The Arts: Intelligent Adaptation of a Novel," Times
     (London), (21 July 1965), 15, col. 1.
          A review of the dramatization of HE by Lance Sieve-
     king and Richard Cottell. The material has been compressed
     and rearranged with skill, preserving much of the dialogue
     and extending certain characters along lines suggested by the
     book. They have not been able, of course, to reproduce the
     "marvellous rich-textured narrative from which the action
     flows." The play was presented at Cambridge.

564. Bateson, F. W. A Guide to English Literature. New
     York: Anchor Books, 1965. Index. p. 191.
          A short bibliography of secondary materials with a
     note that "the best critical study ... so far is probably that
     of Frederick C. Crews."

565. Boyle, Ted E. "Adela Quested's Delusion: The Fail-
     ure of Rationalism in A Passage to India," College
     English, XXVI (March 1965), 478-480.
          The most soluble of all the "enigmatic problems" of
     PI is the significance of Adela's experience in the Marabar
     Caves. To solve it we "need only note EMF's description of
     [her] obviously sexual frustrations prior to the visit to the
     caves and his subtle employment of an unobtrusive symbol--
     the field glasses."

566. Brewster, Dorothy. Doris Lessing. New York: Twayne
     Press, 1965. Index. p. 73.
          A Lessing short story, "Winter in July," revolves
     around EMF's "well-known phrase," a failure to "connect."

567. Brien, Alan. "Living Legends," Vogue, CXLV (Jan
     1965), 124-135+.
          It is rumored that EMF's last book [Arctic Summer]
     is complete and lies in the British Museum awaiting his death
     for publication. Despite the fact that his novels are Edwardi-
     an, they have a special "relevance" to today's generation. He
     is the "laureate of the civilized virtues." Throughout his
     novels two streams run side by side: "muddy melodrama" and
     "crystal-clear comedy."

568. "E. M. Forster," English Literature in Transition,
     VIII, 4 (1965), 278-283.
          An annotated bibliography.

569. Eastman, Richard M. A Guide to the Novel. San
     Francisco: Chandler, 1965. Index. 27, 193-194.

A bibliography of EMF's major works.

570. Erskine-Hill, Howard and Roy Thomas. "A Passage
      to India: Two Points of View," Anglo-Welsh Review, XV
      (Summer 1965), 44-50.
          PI is as much a novel about race as is HE (first
view). In all his novels there are two worlds interacting
positively or negatively upon each other. But PI is more than
a book about racial relations. EMF increases the power
and range of his work through the development of symbolism.

571. Friedman, Alan Howard. "The Turn of the Novel:
      Changes in the Pattern of English Fiction Since 1890 in
      Hardy, Conrad, Forster, and Lawrence," Dissertation
      Abstracts, XXV (1965), 6622.
          EMF's novels provide a tidy and ironic mirror-
image of the traditional shape of experience. His "stream of
conscience" works towards a "climax of progressively nar-
rowing emotional and moral experience which expands, suddenly, to produce his untapered conclusions."

572. Gilbert, S. M. E. M. Forster's A Passage to India
      and Howards End. New York: Monarch, 1965.
          A "study guide." A detailed summary of the plot of
each work with comments. There are also character-analy-
ses and "critical" commentary.

573. Hagopian, John V. "Eternal Moments in the Short Fic-
      tion of E. M. Forster," College English, XXVII (Dec
      1965), 209-215.
          The paper attempts to render "careful definition and
appraisal of EMF's two most distinguished achievements in
short fiction, 'The Road from Colonus' and 'The Eternal
Moment'." In both, the tragic artist is dominant over the
moralist. They present not the "permanent victory of the
race over cruelty and chaos, but rather, as in his 'great'
novels, the pathetic defeat of characters who aspire to his
notion of sainthood, e.g. the aristocracy of the sensitive,
the considerate, and the plucky."

574. Howarth, Herbert. "E. M. Forster and the Contrite
      Establishment," Journal of General Education, XVII
      (Oct 1965), 196-206.
          EMF belongs to the "young humanitarians who, in
turn, belonged to, and felt the onus of belonging to, the
Establishment of 1900." Typical of this group were six men
who launched the Independent Review. EMF's novels are

pervaded by the "ethos" of this group.

575. "Invalids," Times (London), (6 May 1965), 14, col. 7.
      A note to the effect that EMF is recovering from
his stroke.

576. Kilner, G. "Some Questions of Interpretations in 'A
      Passage to India'," Use of English, XVI (Summer 1965),
      302-307.
      The purpose of the article is to attempt to make a
statement of the theme in order to provide a basis for interpretation in terms reliable enough to give reference points
for underlying meanings in the core of the novel.

576A. Kirkpatrick, B[rownlee] J[ean]. A Bibliography of
       E. M. Forster (#19 in The Soho Bibliographies Series).
       London: Rupert Hart-Davis, 1965. [Second edition,
       1968.]

577. Koljević, Svetozar. "E. M. Forster: Sceptic as
      Novelist," Mad River Review, I (Fall-Winter 1965), 3-
      15.
      EMF's vision is largely focused on the "spiritual
barbarity which ... assumes the tyranny of certain ideas to
be legitimate and which, according to EMF, Europe has inherited from Christianity."

578. McDowell, Frederick P. W. "E. M. Forster's Con-
      ception of the Critic," Tennessee Studies in Literature,
      X (1965), 93-100.
      His concept of the critic "faces two ways." He dis-
trusts the critic who does not "reveal a supple sensibility" and
on the other hand "values highly the intellectual and the unin-
tellectual as well as the intuitive."

579. McDowell, Frederick P. W. "Forster's Most Recent
      Critics," English Literature in Transition, VIII, 1 (1965),
      49-62.
      Reviews Wilde's Art and Order--"makes intelligent
use of EMF's uncollected prose; his treatment of the tales is
the most comprehensive to date"; Shahane's E. M. Forster:
A Reassessment, which he calls "the weakest of books on
EMF of a general nature"; Joseph's The Art of Rearrangement;
and Natwar-Singh's E. M. Forster: A Tribute.

580. Martin, John S. "Mrs. Moore and the Marabar Caves:
      A Mythological Reading," Modern Fiction Studies, XI

(Winter 1965-1966), 429-433.

While there are few, if any, overt references to Greek myth in PI, it "seems profitable and plausible" to view Mrs. Moore and the Marabar Caves as "reenactments of Greek mythological archetypes," namely, the celebrated caves of the Cumean Sibyl.

581. "Mr. E. M. Forster Ill," Times (London), (5 May 1965), 12, col. 2.

A note that EMF is seriously ill in Coventry after a stroke. He was visiting the home of a Coventry probation officer when he became ill.

582. Moore, Harry T. E. M. Forster. (Columbia Essays on Modern Writers #10). New York: Columbia University Press, 1965.

EMF has written five novels, two of which are of major importance; a moderate sized volume of collected short stories, and a series of miscellaneous books and articles. His principal writings concern the failure of man to communicate with man satisfactorily, the failure to destroy prejudice, and to establish the relationships that are richly possible. In a wider sense this is the history of humanity in our time.

In his short stories, EMF adopts the guise of fantasy to develop what he says more realistically in his novels. Alex is a "special-interest" book. PP deals with Alexandria again. In effect it is a "continuation of the history-guidebook." Most of the sketches confirm his Hellenism and his dislike of Christianity. At times, they foreshadow the work of Durrell and some are in the "mischievous vein of Anatole France." Aspects is best known for its distinction between flat and round characters. GLD and MT are "acts of piety." MT is a "compelling story," while GLD will catch the interest of those concerned with EMF or with the Cambridge of yesteryear. AH and Two are collections of his critical writings. The essays in AH are principally "belletristic." Two is similar, though its opening section gives the volume somewhat of a different tone. The pieces in that opening section "are dated now." WAFT is closely related to the short stories and later essays. It begins ironically and, as usual, contains a conflict between two worlds: Sawston and Italy. In LJ, the conflict reappears. Of all the characters Stephan alone "seems difficult to accept as actual." RWV is "lighter" than WAFT or LJ. It is a "crowded little comedy" but "less complex and involved" than the first two. Despite its sharpness, however, it "has a thin quality." HE represents a "new" EMF. He had arrived at his major phase as a writer. His

style ranges on the edge of the poetic.   Most of his symbols
are easily discernible, but they embody "that intuitive quality
of the symbolism of the modern school. " EMF had difficulties
with PI for a number of years.   A "piquant" introduction to
these problems and to the setting is given in Hill.   Many interpretations exist, but, as in all of his novels, the "central
theme is the inability of man to connect. "   The action centers
upon an experience of Mrs. Moore and Adela in the Marabar
Caves.   While EMF "never directly says what happened" it is
"safe to assume a religious manifestation. "

583.   "Passage to India, " Bookweek, (15 August 1965), 12.
        A notice of the reissue of PI in paperback (Harvest
Books) with the comment that "this beautifully written account
of a clash of cultures has long since become a classic. "

583A.   Shusterman, David.   The Quest for Certitude in E. M.
        Forster's Fiction.   Bloomington, Ind. : Indiana University
        Press, 1965.
        A not too effective general review of EMF's work.

584.   Tindall, William York.   The Literary Symbol.   Bloom-
        ington, Indiana: Indiana University Press, 1965.   Index.
        pp. 142-144, 189-190.
        Symbolism of actions in the novels of EMF, 147f;
use of rhythm and pattern, 217f; Aspects, 86, 146, 218; HE,
148; PI, 86, 142-144, 189f, 218.

585.   Wimsatt, William K. and Cleanth Brooks.   Literary
        Criticism: A Short History.   New York: Knopf, 1965.
        Index. p. 608.
        A quotation from Anonymity: An Enquiry (London,
1925), p. 14, noting that a "poem points to nothing but itself.
Information is relative--a poem is absolute. "

1966

586.   "Abinger Harvest, " Publisher's Weekly, CXC (29 Aug
        1966), 348.
        A notation of the publication of AH in paperback
(Harvest Books) and an indication that the collection of essays
is "wide-ranging and consistently interesting. "

587.   Bradbury, Malcolm, ed.   Forster: A Collection of
        Critical Essays (Twentieth Century Views).   Englewood
        Cliffs, New Jersey: Prentice-Hall, 1966.

The essays range from "fairly early commentaries" to recent, more "analytical essays." Until recently, EMF was regarded as an "interesting" novelist, but not quite a major writer. Recent criticism, however, has taken another approach. It has "demonstrated" that he is "more complex and more modern than the earlier views allow."

    I. Richards, I. A. "A Passage to Forster: Reflections on a Novelist," see #73.

    II. Burra, Peter. "The Novels of E. M. Forster," see #104.

    III. Leavis, F. R. "E. M. Forster," see #279.

    IV. Warren, Austin. "E. M. Forster," reprinted as Chapter VII, in Rage for Order. see: #236.

    V. Savage, Derek S. "E. M. Forster."

    VI. Trilling, Lionel. "Forster and the Liberal Tradition." The introduction to Trilling's E. M. Forster. see: #189.

    VII. Waggoner, Hyatt Howe. "Notes on the Uses of Coincidence in the Novels of E. M. Forster." see #201.

    VIII. Kermode, Frank. "Mr. E. M. Forster as a Symbolist." see: #494 ("The One Orderly Product").

    IX. Crews, Frederick C. "E. M. Forster's Comic Spirit." see: #485 (Chapter XII)

    X. Smith, H. A. "Forster's Humanism and the Nineteenth Century." Discusses the nature of the opposition to Sawston, namely "two humanisms," one romantic, the other rational.

    XI. Bradbury, Malcolm. "E. M. Forster's Howards End." see: #481.

    XII. Brown, E. K. "Rhythm in E. M. Forster's A Passage to India." see: #247.

    XIII. Parry, Benita. "Passage to More than India." EMF concerns himself with questions about which society more effectively satisfies man's quest for certainty and revelation, but his answers are neither confident nor entirely spiritual. The novel has a deep social and historical sense.

588. Carens, James F. The Satiric Art of Evelyn Waugh. Seattle and London: University of Washington Press, 1966. Index. p. 138.

    Waugh's Black Mischief and Scoop, satires of empire, are "subtly different" from PI because, though Waugh ridiculed imperialism, he is not hostile to it as EMF in his novel.

589. Connolly, Cyril. The Modern Movement: One Hundred Key Books from England, France and America, 1800-

<u>1950.</u> New York: Atheneum, 1966. pp. 28, 50.
LJ is one of the key books of the modern period,
1880-1920. PI is a great book of the twenties in which EMF
"explored the limitations of humanism."

590. Daleski, H. M. "Rhythmic and Symbolic Patterns in
<u>A Passage to India,</u>" in Shalvi, Alice and A. A. Mendilow,
eds. <u>Studies in English Language and Literature XVII</u>
(Hebrew University, Jerusalem), 1966. pp. 258-279.
The rhythmic movement of the novel implies that
human relations are subject to the same kind of ineluctable
rhythms as the cosmos. This is linked to the "symbolic
pattern ... the action ... that leads in turn to each of the
stages in the rhythmic process initiated in or near the mosque,
cave, and temple, which are themselves symbolic of the tendencies exemplified in or near them." The symbolic pattern
is the "ground of the rhythmic pattern." The article continues
in an attempt to "establish the effectiveness of the overall design."

591. Friedman, Alan. <u>The Turn of the Novel.</u> New York:
Oxford University Press, 1966. Index. pp. 106-129.
PI, 116-129; RWV, 29, 108-112; Aspects, 106; HE, 28,
113, 200n.; WAFT, 113-115.
When EMF speaks of "expansion" as the "idea the
novelist must cling to" he is referring not to an "open structure" but rather to the "total final effect on the reader, the
after-effects of his reading." This position is reflected in
his novels. (see also: #571. The volume is a published dissertation).

592. Friend, Robert. "The Theme of Salvation in 'The Point
of It'," in Shalvi, Alice and A. A. Mendilow, eds.
<u>Studies in English Language and Literature XVI</u> (Hebrew
University, Jerusalem). pp. 243-257.
EMF's basic intentions are "religious and didactic."
The story poses the question "how am I to be saved?"
Micky's inability to see the point of salvation "defines his
damnation." How he makes the journey to salvation is "what
the story is about."

593. Goldman, Mark. "Virginia Woolf and E. M. Forster:
A Critical Dialogue," <u>Texas Studies in Language and
Literature</u>," VII (1966), 387-400.
EMF and VW represent two basically opposing views
in a recurring critical dialectic on the novel. She saw the
need for the "writer to capture the sensibility or reality of his

age." This led to her emphasis on experimentation. She criticized EMF for "trying to capture the Georgian sensibility without abandoning the Edwardian form."

594. Heilbrun, Carolyn. "Speaking of Books: A Modern Among Contemporaries," New York Times Book Review, (30 Jan 1966), 2.
      We are beginning to believe that almost everything that happened in the first half of the 20th century in art and literature began in the thirteen years and seven months which are called the "Edwardian Age." It was the last time of simple happiness when progress appeared possible and scientific salvation assured. But not all believed that this was so. James, Conrad and EMF did not. WAFT is not a "big" work; getting through it is an effortless task. Its title is prophetic. Trilling is annoyed because EMF refuses to be great. EMF is the first to have faced and honored the "claims of sexuality." Few of his contemporaries had his vision. Few saw that a "loss of the old commandments," celebrated in their books, left an "order more complete." EMF not only experienced the modern vision a good deal earlier than others but retained it longer.

595. Hoare, Dorothy M. "E. M. Forster," in Studies in the Modern Novel. Port Washington, New York: Kennikat Press, 1966. pp. 68-96.
      EMF's early writings owe a debt to Meredith, but he goes beyond Meredithian themes. All through his work, he contrasts and brings together the romantic and the ironic views and makes clear his preference for the romantic.

596. Hunt, John D. "Muddle and Mystery in A Passage to India," ELH, XXXIII (Dec 1966), 497-517.
      There are many difficulties in "defining this elusive novel." First, it is all too often read as an "obvious and automatic successor to the previous four; whereas ... it represents a real change in EMF's concerns." Second, the final section yields little consistently fruitful material for examination in relation to the previous sections ... yet the whole momentum ... culminates in the Hindu festival ... the dominant impression of the final section ... is its muddle," which EMF "manages successfully to evoke" yet "runs dangerously close to reducing his own novel to a shambles." This "celebration of disorder" is a "paradoxical effort for a novelist ... committed to notions of aesthetic form. This paradox ... is due to the reading of the novel."

597. Jacobson, Dan. "Forster's Cave," New Statesman,
     LXXII (14 Oct 1966), 560.
         EMF's skepticism is very far from a "purely nega-
tive or corrosive force" in PI. It is, rather, the "essential,
impersonal medium in which all the actions of the novel take
place." It also controls the "eloquent descriptions."

598. Leary, Daniel. "The Cave and the Mountain by Wilfrid
     Stone" (review), Catholic World, CCIII (Sept 1966), 373-
     374.
         Not since Trilling has so "thoughtful a treatment of
[EMF] appeared." Stone makes it clear that EMF was one of
the "truly significant writers of the twentieth century." The
review then describes the contents of the book.

599. "Liberal Prophet," Times (London), (30 June 1966), 16,
     col. 3.
         A review of Stone's The Cave and the Mountain. The
author approaches EMF in a spirit of "eager inquiry ... his
purpose is neither to exault nor debunk. He is a cool, ap-
praising judge." This is an "admirable study."

600. "Looking In: A Skillful Piece of Bridging," Times
     (London), (16 Feb 1966), 17, col. 6.
         A review of the Hart dramatization of WAFT. It was
televised on the BBC I program, "The Play of the Month,"
15 Feb. The play was deservedly successful on the stage
though it "missed much of EMF's subtlety of tone." It is
equally successful on TV.

601. Lucas, John. "Wagner and Forster: Parsifal and A
     Room with a View," ELH, XXXIII (March 1966), 92-117.
         RWV takes its meaning from the truths embodied in
Wagner's work by presenting a basic opposition of pagan and
Christian as holy and devilish; Parsifal works by presenting
a basic opposition of pagan and Christian as devilish and
holy. EMF's "good" people have the same motives as
Wagner's, i.e. to "defend life itself." The characters owe
their "mystic" status to their author's "availing himself"
of the structures of oppositions in Wagner's work.

602. McDowell, Frederick P. W. "E. M. Forster: Recent
     Extended Studies," English Literature in Transition, IX,
     3 (1966), 156-168.
         Kirkpatrick's bibliography is "unlikely to be super-
seded." [N. B. It was by a second edition in 1968.]
Moore's E. M. Forster [#584] advances the study of EMF "less

than even a pamphlet of this sort should." Bradbury's
Forster: A Collection of Critical Essays should prove to be
useful [#587]. Shusterman's The Quest for Certitude is not
as illuminating as Wilde's Art and Order [#558]. Stone's
The Cave and the Mountain "will produce varying reactions
among Forsterians."

603. McDowell, Frederick P. W. "E. M. Forster's Theory
      of Literature," Criticism, VIII (Winter 1966), 19-43.
      EMF is no systematic critic but he has written a
number of theoretical essays and, since 1924, many articles
and essays which touch upon theory. Rigid principles are
lacking, though there are certain "presuppositions" which
underly his impressionism, i.e. the artist is a "god-like"
creator; the author's philosophical reflection must grow out
of his materials; the prime character of a work is internal
order, etc.

604. Mendilow, A. A. "The Triadic World of E. M.
      Forster," in Shalvi, Alice and A. A. Mendilow, eds.
      Studies in English Language and Literature, XVII (Hebrew
      University, Jerusalem) 1966.
      The "tripartite structure" of PI is determined by
three symbols: the mosque, the caves, and the temple, which
are "ambivalent in meaning" and, like India, are "difficult and
equivocal." This indicates, perhaps "some uncertainty in the
values and attitudes of EMF." This ambiguity applies also to
his treatment of the main characters.

605. Mukkherjee, Sujit. "The Marabar Mystery: An Addi-
      tion to the Case-Book on the Caves." College English,
      XXVII (March 1966), 501-503.
      Whatever may be the symbolic "doctrine" of the
caves, they have had in actuality no association with the
theory and practice of Hinduism. The originals--the Barabar
Caves--were associated with the Ajivika sect whose doctrine
of destiny was that "all change and movement were illusory
and that the world was in reality eternally and immovably at
rest." It is difficult to ignore the reactions of the Western-
ers who in their reactions reflect these basic tenets of Ajivika
belief.

606. Natwar-Singh, K. "The Cave and the Mountain by
      Wilfred Stone" (review), Saturday Review (NY), XLIX
      (5 March 1966), 43.
      The reviewer quarrels with Stone's emphasis on
symbolism in EMF's work. EMF, he says, "needs no props."

607. Raina, M. L. "Forster Parallel in Lawrence's 'St. Maur'," Notes and Queries (London), XIII (March 1966), 96-97.

There is some resemblance between Mrs. Moore's experience in PI and the vision of Lou Witt in Lawrence's "St. Maur" which was published in 1925 a year after EMF's book. It is likely that Lawrence's reactions to the EMF novel may have gone into the rendering of the incident.

608. Rau, Santha Rama. "Oranges, Birds and Crystals," Reporter, XXXIV (24 March 1966), 54+.

A review of Stone's The Cave and the Mountain. The reviewer is automatically "prejudiced in favor of anyone who gives such profound attention and scholarship" to EMF. Stone explores a "developing myth," EMF's "private view of the human predicament."

609. Rosenthal, M. L. "Only Connect," Spectator (23 Sept 1966), 383-384.

Review of Stone's The Cave and the Mountain. Stone is a "truly sensitive literary scholar, [who] knows that ... [EMF's books] speak rather beautifully for themselves. The critic need only ... point to aspects here and there," "sometimes Professor Stone clarifies superbly."

610. Scholes, Roker, ed. Approaches to the Novel. San Francisco: Chandler, 1966.

Reprints Chapter V of Aspects. Scholes summarizes EMF's positions and notes that, like Stephen Crane, EMF is willing to assume that "plot" exists and must be discussed in connection with character. EMF, however, associates character with life and plot with art.

611. Scott, Paul. "How Well Have They Worn? --1--A Passage to India," Times (London), (6 Jan 1966), 15.

The failure of "Fieldingism," i.e. "liberal humanism" and the "self-awareness of failure as inevitable but darkly mysterious [is what] makes PI not only one of the great tragic works of twentieth century fiction but one that we have still not wholly grown into, let alone grown out of."

612. Shipley, John B. "Additions to the E. M. Forster Bibliography," Bibliographical Society of America Papers, LX (April 1966), 224-225.

Offers additions to the "Addenda" section of Kirkpatrick's bibliography of EMF using the same tabulation. Lists six additional works and additional information not supplied by her in her bibliography.

613. Stone, Wilfred. The Cave and the Mountain, A Study
      of E. M. Forster. Stanford, Calif.: Stanford Universi-
      ty Press, 1966.
          Chapter I Introduction: Poetry and Prose. EMF is a
Coleridgean. Nearly all of his characters are either Bentha-
mites or Coleridgeans, opposing the mind to the heart, the
letter to the spirit, efficiency to love. He is convinced that
poetry must be joined to prose if we are to survive. His
doctrine is Art with a capital A. Art to him is an "idea of
wholeness." His only continuously productive period as an
artist was between 1902-1912. PI was an "Indian Summer" of
a talent which showed weariness before WWI. His art dried
up because "events ... moved too fast for him." The passing of the countryside and the passing of the Victorian family
were two events which hurt his artistic powers. To understand
EMF "a sense of loss, of partial disinheritance" is necessary.
          Chapter 2. Clapham: The Father's House. EMF is
an "ancestor-worshipper" who "longs for" the presence of his
ancestors as something needed in his own character. The
archetype-ancestor is Henry Thornton, his great-grandfather
and a leading figure in the Clapham sect. The sect was a
group of practical, intelligent and wealthy Evangelical reform-
ers who flourished from 1790-1835 and achieved a great deal
of good. EMF is a "relativist" who is longing for the absolutes that the group never questioned. He also sought their
"tight, little coterie" in the coteries of Cambridge and Bloomsbury. He maintained that the "clique" is a "valuable social
device," but only if it is "little." The little society also appeals to him because he is "homeless." Though he was
drawn to the Clapham Sect, he found that its greatest defect
was its "indifference to the unseen." To its members,
"poetry, mystery, passion, ecstasy, music, don't count."
These things do count to EMF.
          Chapter 3. The Apostolic Ring. To understand EMF
one must go to the Apostles, a secret discussion society at
Cambridge, which he joined about 1897. It was through this
society that he entered Bloomsbury. He had found a "little
society" within a "little society." The Apostles displayed a
"monogeniety of spirit." The members were members for
life and its ritual remained relatively unchanged. The society
gave him a "footing" independent of Clapham "upon which he
could negotiate with those formidable ancestors. The contrast
between Clapham and the Apostles which dramatizes the conflict between prose and poetry, the Benthamite and Coleridgean
conflict, is "crucial for an understanding of EMF's intellectual
and artistic development." Nathaniel Wedd is one of the

Apostles who most influenced him. He "awakened EMF to
the classics," and stimulated his "sense of mockery and
humor." In Dickinson, EMF found an "idol to worship," but
Wedd "encouraged" EMF to write.

Chapter 4. Goldsworthy Lowes Dickinson. EMF's
biography of him is a labor of love, the payment of a fra-
ternal debt as MT was the payment of a filial debt. EMF's
partisanship shows on every page. No other book reveals
his capacity for hero-worship. It is difficult, however, to
understand GLD's influence on minds superior to his own
when one reads his books. He was a homosexual and tried
to write about it in mythological form in an obscure book,
The Magic Flute. EMF tried to write his own myth in LJ.
He shares most of GLD's ideas and ideals but brings to them
a style "touched with gaiety, astringency, and irony."

Chapter 5. Forster's Esthetics: From Words to
Music. His ideas on art do not amount to an esthetic but
are connected with one. His main contribution is to bring the
novel within its range of consideration. His effort in
Aspects is to elevate the novel to Art. Most of his ideas
on the arts are found in "Anonymity." The work of art is
an objective reality and the creative state of mind is its
subjective or psychological form; the binding force is love.
It is the Trinity in non-Christian terms. The experience of
art is an end in itself. Its poetic value is in this intrinsic
worth alone. The internal order and harmony of a work of
art is a kind of rhythm which stitches it together and shapes
it. Art is not a part or copy of the real world, but a world
by itself. Art ought to be appreciated on two levels because
it has a double existence. It exists as a work produced by an
individual capable of being named, and out of something that
it has in common with all other deeper personalities. This
is one of EMF's most critical statements. Literature is an
organization of words that conveys something beyond information. Aspects applies these general ideas to the novel.

Chapter 6. The Stones: Fantasy. EMF's fiction
"describes a transition from the subjective to the objective.
His short stories are youthful productions dealing with the
problems of youth. They "are awkward, self-conscious, and
amateurish." They record the first stage of rebellion which
PI completes. His stories are fantasies because he has some
"scandal" to hide, i.e. the "scandalous act of cutting the
silver cord, of biting the feeding hand." Fantasy is a "make-
belief," the "creation of a myth"; it tends to dramatize a
"humanist religion."

Chapter 7. Where Angels Fear to Tread. It is a
"gay book, boldly and simply plotted." Its plot is a comic

and contrived sequence of cause-and-effect relationships
based upon an irregular marriage. The most interesting
aspect of the book is the ambiguities in its comedy. It
"hovers between comedy and prophecy."

   Chapter 8. The Longest Journey: The Slaughter of
the Innocents. The novel demonstrates more clearly than any
other of EMF's novels the "war between his moral and
esthetic impulses." It is "confused" but "fascinating." It is
flawed because the "forces of anti-literature drain its strength."
These forces derive from its "mixed motives." It is the
portrait of the artist, but also the portrait of the non-artist.
As the book is confused in its purpose, so too is Rickie. He
is tested in three phases and the book has three parts. The
division is fairly common in EMF's works. On the whole,
the book "does not succeed."

   Chapter 9. A Room with a View: Sex and Sensibility.
EMF's fiction is "essentially an experiment in self-confi-
dence." The book provides a "metaphor" which "illumines a
pervasive theme" in his fiction. It is his most objective
work. The book represents not a new departure for him, but
a "cleaning up of old business." The first half recalls the
manner of WAFT; the second, WAFT with "the breath of LJ
blowing through it." Part II explains Part I. The two
dramatize, rather sharply, the author's desire to wear "a
comic mask and let us see behind it." It is the only one of
EMF's books in which "the problem of continuance is met in
a straight-forward sexual way."

   Chapter 10. Howards End: Red-bloods and Molly-
coddles. HE represents a broadening of EMF's subject from
a "private to a public world." The book is a test of Bloomsbury liberalism and its ability to survive a "marriage with
the world." The motto of Margaret, "who speaks for EMF,"
is "only connect." In this, EMF is testing not only a moral
thesis, but "himself." All of the book's experiments in
connection are "symbolic testings" of that "slippery walk
between decadence and brutality, ivory-towerism and con-
centration camps ... which has been the road of modern
history." EMF takes shelter in female bodies and fights out
his theme through them. Howards End is a symbolic house;
it is the most important house in the book and "represents
all of England and its spiritual inheritance." The question of
the book is "who shall inherit England?" and the plot is about
"the rights of property." The key rhythms are the "dominant
phases of Margaret and Helen." From them, the main themes
expand "like rings in water." The book is "full of symbols."

   Chapter 11. A Passage to Alexandria. EMF's so-
journs in the Middle East and in India mark stages in his

maturation as a writer. By the time he reached Alexandria,
the need for fantasy was gone. This period must be considered
if we are "to account for the relative failure of HE and the
... achievement of PI." The chief work of this period is
Alex. It is "charming" and perhaps one of "the few genuinely
good things he was able to do in that period between 1914 and
1924." PP is a more direct anticipation of PI than is Alex.
It shows him as the "historical biographer" at "the top of his
form." Both books are turned into "humanistic arguments."
Between 1920 and 1922, he reviewed many books on history,
politics, anthropology, biography, etc.
      Chapter 12. A Passage to India: The Great Round.
EMF's fiction is filled with the basic symbols of circles,
containers, etc. These "feminine" images operate in "double
roles as persons and as paradises." His work shows an
awareness that "life lives on death." PI is an attempt to "relate the broken circles of his own experience to some final
scheme of ultimate value." Its fundamental structure consists
of "circle after circle." The basic circle is the Marabar
Caves and the entire novel is "implied" in their description.
The book is divided into three sections which correspond to
the Indian Year: cool spring, hot summer, wet monsoon of
autumn. They also suggest Moslem, Anglo-Indian [N. B.
English], and Hindu, and the qualities of character and temperament associated with these groups. The novel is a masterpiece of understanding. It shows us the context in terms
of which "all questions must be asked and all questions
answered."
      Chapter 13. Criticism: The Near and the Far. PI
does not mark an end to EMF's work but a turning point. He
did not want to continue to write novels and he hasn't for
some forty years. Since 1924, he has published some four
hundred pieces. Though theme and subject vary, all are
marked by a "unique sensibility and style." It is not easy,
however, to find a unifying thread running through his literary
criticism, which is often "brilliant" but sometimes "astonishingly irresponsible."

614. Tanner, Tony. "Selected Books," London Magazine, VI
     (Aug 1966), 102-109.
      A review of Stone's The Cave and the Mountain.
Stone sets out to answer the following questions: "What is the
nature of EMF's wisdom? what are his values and where did
they come from; at what point do they reveal their inade-
quacies and limitations?" His work is "certainly the most
comprehensive, and arguably the best study of EMF to have
appeared so far.

615. Thomson, George H. "A Note on the Snake Imagery
      of A Passage to India," English Literature in Transition,
      IX, 2 (1966), 108-110.
          The theme of the presence and the absence of God is
reflected in the snake imagery. The development, it must
be noted, is in many respects "non-theological."

1967

616. Baugh, Albert C., ed. A Literary History of England.
      Second edition. New York: Appleton-Century-Crofts,
      1967. Index. p. 1569.
          The most widely read of EMF's novels is PI. Its
fame is in part due to "considerations adventitious to its
high merits in style, pattern, characterization and atmosphere." Veins of "quietism and symbolism" run through his
books with a constantly recurring contrast between the inner
and the outer life. Episodes of melodramatic violence suddenly interrupt passages of delicate psychological analysis.

617. Bell, Vereen M. "Comic Seriousness in A Passage to
      India," South Atlantic Quarterly, LXVI (Autumn 1967),
      606-617.
          Criticism of EMF has, of recent years, overlooked
the fact that PI is a very funny novel as well as a serious one.
One of his distinctions is his ability to move fluently from
"shrewd social comedy" to the "most exacting kind of metaphysical speculation."

617A. Colmer, John. E. M. Forster: A Passage to India.
      (#30, Studies in English Literature). London: Arnold,
      1967.
          A study guide which covers such topics as "What
kind of a novel is it?" and "What is its meaning and value?"

618. Costa, Richard Hauer. H. G. Wells. New York:
      Twayne, 1967. Index. pp. 65, 116, 150.
          Wells was "spiritual godfather" to EMF's "The
Machine Stops." Wells's novels of society enabled writers
like EMF to turn their attentions to "more engrossing psychological aspects."

619. "E. M. Forster 'Poor' After Fall," New York Times,
      (10 Jan 1967), 10, col. 6.
          Cambridge, Eng., 9 Jan. After a fall, EMF was
rushed to a hospital. His condition is said to be "rather
poor."

620. Edwards, Michael. British India 1772-1947: A Survey
      of the Nature and Effects of Alien Rule. New York:
      Taplinger, 1967.
         PI is as "offensive as other books on India." EMF
shows an inability to understand the Indian or the world of the
British in India.

621. Holroyd, Michael. Lytton Strachey, A Critical Bi-
      ography. Vol. I: The Unknown Years 1880-1910.
      London: Heinemann, 1967. Index.
         Weekend trips to Cambridge, 123; description of
EMF, 129-130; influence of Nathaniel Wedd upon EMF, 168n;
biography of GLD, 173, 421; his nickname, 205; quoted on
Cambridge, 328, 421; pen-portrait of Lytton, 316; and the
Independent Review, 353; "pseudo scholarship," 375; member
of Bloomsbury group, 411, 416, 418; tea and beer, 413, 423.

622. Holroyd, Michael. Lytton Strachey, A Critical
      Biography. Vol. II. The Years of Achievement. Lon-
      don: Heinemann, 1967. Index.
         On pension life in Italy, 80, 86; "a mediocre man,"
106; visits Strachey at the Lacket, 148; acts as valet and
porter, 149; at Tidmarsh, 370, 457; in Bloomsbury, 486;
with J. R. Ackerley at Ham Spray, 515; his feelings for
Ralph Partridge, 517, 520; visits Strachey at Ham Spray,
531-532, 575; his book and Edwin Muir's, 510; critical
opinion of Elizabeth and Essex, 614; shines as required,
645-646; introduces Strachey to a "human weasel," 655;
letters to Strachey, 141n.

623. Kreuzer, James R. and Lee Cogan. Studies in Prose
      Writing. Alternate Edition, Revised. New York: Holt,
      Rinehart, and Winston, 1967. Index. pp. 298-304.
         A reprint of part of EMF's "The Ivory Tower"
(Atlantic, Jan. 1939), with stylistic analysis.

624. Legouis, Emile, Louis Cazamian, and Raymond Lee
      Vergnas. A History of English Literature. New York:
      Macmillan, 1967. Index. pp. 1370-1372.
         Beneath his "free and easy manner" lurks "an artist
deeply concerned with his performance." Sexuality appears
to be of no importance in his novels. The real and wise
heroines have left it behind.

625. McDonald, Walter E. "Forster's A Passage to India,"
      Explicator, XXV (March 1967), item #54.
         EMF does not tell us what has happened to Adela in

the cave because it "enforces her theme of unresolved tension, ambivalence, and suspicion."

626.   Magnus, John.   "Ritual Aspects of E. M. Forster's
        The Longest Journey," Modern Fiction Studies, XIII
        (Summer 1967), 195-210.
           The tripartite structure of LJ and PI reflects the
different spiritual states of the characters as they develop in
the novels.   The titles of the different parts of PI suggest that
the passage from one of these states to another entails a
ritual.   His short stories also display the same ritualistic
elements.   The most significant fact about these rituals is that
they work.   Every significant transformation of a character is
attended by overt ritual or at least by "ritual symbolism."   In
LJ ritual transformation is brought more freely into the con-
sciousness of the characters than in HE.   One of the many
complex systems which operate throughout the book is
Stephan's numerous "water-rituals."   Rickie's own sensitivity
to ritual is so acute that it pervades virtually everything.   If
one ignores the ritualistic structure of LJ, the plot must appear
as episodic or at best, loosely constructed.

627.   "Mr. E. M. Forster," Times (London), (11 Jan 1957),
        5, col. 5.
           A note to the effect that EMF, 88, was taken to
Addenbrooke's New Hospital, Cambridge, after a fall in his
rooms at King's.   He is reported as slightly improved at
night.

628.   "Mr. E. M. Forster," Times (London), (2 Jan 1967),
        9, col. 7.
           A note to the effect that EMF's condition is slightly
improved after his fall.   see: #627.

629.   Pritchett, V. S.   "Mr. Forster's Birthday," in The
        Living Novel and Later Appreciations.   New York:
        Random House, 1967.   pp. 244-250.
           EMF has survived as a novelist by "interposing" by a
"misleading slackness, by the refusal to speak in a public
voice.   This has given the personal a startling strength."

630.   Schmerl, Rudolf B.   "Fantasy as Technique," Virginia
        Quarterly Review, XLII (Autumn 1967), 644-656.
           EMF's essay on fantasy in Aspects illuminates almost
all of its relevant elements without quite defining it.

631.   Shahane, V. A.   "Forster's A Passage to India, Chapter

VII," Explicator, XXVI (Dec 1967), item #36.
Godbole's song is neither comic nor ironic; it is
"deeply imbued with religious and mystical significance" and
"makes its own contribution to the ultimate meaning of the
novel."

631A.   Shahane, V. A.   "A Visit to Mr. E. M. Forster,
Quest (Bombay), LIII (1967), 43-46.

631B.   Stevenson, Lionel.   The History of the English Novel:
Yesterday and After.   New York: Barnes and Noble, 1967.
Index.
Pages 87-102, 103, 111, 142, 160, 223, 230, 232,
235, 275, 290, 297, 299, 311, 364, 369, 372, and many
passim references.   Aspects: 101, 102; Celest: 98; HE, 95,
97; LJ: 92-93, 94; PI: 99-102; RWV: 93-95; WAFT: 90-91, 93.

632.   Trilling, Lionel.   E. M. Forster, A Study.   New and
Revised Edition.   London: Hogarth Press, 1967.
There are two reasons for a new edition of this work:
EMF has added to the canon of his work since the appearance
of the first edition, and a formidable body of criticism has
grown up.   Neither reason, however, has caused Trilling to
change his essential views.   For this new edition the bibliography has been "at least partially" brought up to date and
"literal or factual errors" in the text have been corrected.
Further, since the first edition, Trilling has become EMF's
friend.   see also #189.
I.   Introduction: Forster and the Liberal Imagination.   EMF is the only living novelist who gives one the sense
of having learned something each time one reads his work.
His manner is comic, owing much to Fielding, Dickens,
Meredith, and James.   His plots are always sharp and definitive.
He expresses difference by means of struggle and struggle by
means of open conflict.   EMF has been long committed to the
liberal tradition, yet he is "deeply at odds with the liberal
mind."   The indifference to the commonplace of liberal
thought makes the very texture of his novels.
II.   Sawston and Cambridge.   A summary of EMF's
life is given.   He was schooled at Tonbridge which is the
Sawston of his first two novels.   It stands as the stronghold
of "genteel, snobbish philistinism."   It gave him his great
theme of the "undeveloped heart."   Cambridge taught him to
deal with Sawston.
III.   The Short Stories: A Statement of Themes.
The Greek Myths made too deep an impression on EMF.   Those
not in the "genre of mythical fantasy" endure the best.   His

mythology is inappropriate to his themes.

IV. Where Angels Fear to Tread. It is a novel of
learning and growth and broken ties, of questioning, of dis-
illusionment and conversion, of criticism of the middle class,
of sexuality. Its theme is the effect of a strong culture and
a foreign country upon provincial personalities. It begins as
a comedy of manners, becomes fierce and melodramatic, and
ends in enlightened despair.

V. The Longest Journey. It is the least perfect of
EMF's novels, but perhaps his "most brilliant, most dramatic, and the most passionate." Nevertheless, it "flies
apart."

VI. A Room with a View. The novel has affinities
with WAFT though it is smaller in scale and tone. In it,
EMF compromises on whether the world is good or evil.
This uncertainty points out moral judgments which will "haunt"
EMF's intellectual life.

VII. Howards End. It is "undoubtedly" EMF's
"masterpiece." It develops to the fullest the themes and attitudes embodied in the earlier books. It is a novel about
England's fate, and a story about the latent class war. The
story moves the symbols. The house is the symbol for
England. The plot is about the rights of property and it asks
the question, "Who shall inherit England?" The class struggle is entirely within the middle class, with Bast at the lower
end and the Schlegels at the upper. Ruth Wilcox dominates
the novel. Margaret is the heroine of the practical life;
Helen that of the ideal, and Helen's child is the symbol of
"the classless life."

VIII. A Passage to India. It is EMF's most conventional and comfortable book. It is his least surprising
novel, the least capricious and least personal. The theme of
separation underlies every relationship in it. It is not about
India alone but about all of life.

IX. Mind and Will: Forster's Literary Criticism.
EMF is not a great critic. He has an aversion to raising up
barriers and setting up categories. He is a critic with no
"drive to consistency." He is impressionistic. There are
many wrong judgments in Aspects, yet it is "full of the finest
perceptions." He has faith in the order which the intellect
can bring. He has an intense "wisftulness" for the "slovenly
East" and the "primitive and non-progressive community."

633. Wiley, Paul L. "E. M. Forster," Wisconsin Studies
     in Contemporary Literature, VIII (Summer 1967), 459-462.
         A review of Shusterman's The Quest for Certitude in
E. M. Forster's Fiction. The study suggests that EMF is

"more or less old hat. "

634. Woolf, Leonard Sidney. Downhill All the Way: An
        Autobiography of the Years 1919-1939. London:
        Hogarth Press, 1967. Index. pp. 107, 114, 130.
        Speaks of EMF at Monks House [Leonard and Vir-
ginia Woolf's weekend retreat]. He also recounts the early
Bloomsbury group which included EMF, and EMF's connection with the Nation, of which LW was literary editor.

                                1968

635. Brander, Laurence. E. M. Forster: A Critical
        Study. London: Rupert Hart-Davis, 1968.
        Introduction. EMF's novels are essentially Ed-
wardian. They are social history as well as studies of the
Edwardian mind. He is a humanist who cares passionately
for the intelligence. Friendship, he holds, is the only reliable thing. Some of his best work was done in celebration
of friends. Essentially he is a traditionalist. He has the
"preacher's itch. "
        "Goldie. " An examination of GLD which is "really
a celebration of Cambridge. " Brander finds it difficult to
examine EMF's work without "copious quotations. " He
does so carefully, reviewing the different parts of the biography. In it, Brander sees "the magic quality of great
verse. "
        The Hill of Devi. The book is the result of EMF's
attempt to understand the Indian mind, and his involvement in
the life of the state. His descriptions are "uniquely wonderful. " Hill is the best travel book on India in English. Two
personal themes emerge: his affection for the prince and his
sense of the burden of inefficiency he was unable to alleviate.
The book's "technical brilliance" is great. His chief desire,
as in GLD, is to bring his subject alive.
        Marianne Thornton. Much of MT is the subject's own
work, but again, the subject "comes to life. "
        Alexandria and Pharos and Pharillon. He did not
produce a "great history" of Alexandria, but a "good deal of
journalism" and a guidebook with an historical preface which
is "one of the most perfect things EMF has given us. " His
gift of "imaginative vision" is well displayed. These books
have been generally ignored by the critics, which is strange
because they "develop attitudes towards human thinking about
religion which are at the centre of EMF's greatest novel. "
        Aspects of the Novel. In the work is an idea of the

novel which "will stand beside the great celebrations of the
epic form." Brander then summarizes its contents.

Where Angels Fear to Tread. The novel makes fun
of suburbia and questions the values he was to question very
seriously in later novels. England is Sawston; Monteriano,
Italy. Englishmen become "sentient" when they come into
contact with Italy. Gino's pain on the death of his son makes
him emerge into "a round character."

Room with a View. Mr. Emerson is a "real person."
In a curious sense, the novel is a "love story." This and
WAFT are two novels which would have been "very slight
sketches" without Gino and the Emersons. These characters
"foretell the books to come." This is EMF's last novel in
the comic manner. He would not return to comedy because
he "was concerned about society and mankind."

The Longest Journey. The novel is an example of
the young novelist experimenting with the form, but with a
theme more serious than in the first two novels. EMF develops "the spirit of place." Cambridge is where truth is
pursued intellectually; Wiltshire, where truth appears in nature and the nature of things; and Sawston is the place of
hypocrisy and pretence. The story is simple. The action
is not so much story as conflict. The reflections are mature,
but the outlook of the observer is young. The women characters are not agreeable. The management of the Wiltshire
section is a "technical triumph." EMF's prose has "hints
of ... magic in it." The characters are, however, not
"amiable" and their conflicts are not "very absorbing."

Howards End. The themes of the novel: personal
relationships and the influence of someone dead; the celebration of England in quiet word-patterns; the flux and instability
of the city contrasted to sane living in the country in houses
like Howards End. Ruth Wilcox dominates all the other
characters; she has the Forsterian virtues of tolerance and
sympathy, and receives her strength from Howards End.
The relationships between Margaret and Helen produce the
greatest scenes in the book. Leonard Bast is the most
baffling character. This complicated novel gives the impression of having been composed in "white heat." Howards End
stands for understanding and peace. The philosophical comments are mature. If EMF had not written PI, HE would be
called his masterpiece.

Passage to India. The novel has its prophetic theme,
the modern theme, of friendship between people of different
races. Its deeper theme is a probing for truth. Aziz is
central to the story as is Gino in his first novel. The value
of PI lies in its "poetical quality," the "natural descriptions,

and the entry into the minds of the central characters."
    The Short Stories. They do not have strong story
lines, but all show an "enquiring mind" which often postulates
a situation that seems impossible so that it can be made ac-
ceptable. There is "lively and nimble fancy in all and a surprising amount of cruelty and violence."
    Abinger Harvest. The pieces are "mostly journalism."
There is no elaborate design in the collection nor any cumu-
lative impact. The writer is a humanist.
    Two Cheers for Democracy. Mostly broadcasts and
lectures. The collection has greater impact than AH because
the pieces "fuse into an unusual picture of a human mind during a crisis in human affairs."

636. Doyle, Paul A. Sean O'Faolain. New York: Twayne,
    1968. Index. p. 128.
    O'Faolain considered EMF to be "blessed with a
talent for quiet raillery."

637. Fagan, B. W. "Forster and His Publishers," Book-
    seller, (28 Dec 1968), 2070-2072.
    Fagan was a junior partner in the firm of E. Arnold
and Co. when EMF brought in the manuscript of PI. From
1930, Fagan handled all of his books. EMF always held to his
views firmly and used no literary agent. Fagan describes a
law suit against EMF upon the publication of AH in 1936. The
offending essay was withdrawn and the volume reissued.

638. "Forster at 90," Times (London), (20 Dec 1968), 8,
    col. 7.
    A note to the effect that King's College, Cambridge,
is preparing to celebrate his ninetieth birthday quietly with
a small luncheon party and a college concert on Sunday,
26 January 1969, for which he has chosen the program. The
Cambridge Humanists will have a tea party in his honor, 25
Jan.

639. Furbank, P. N. "Tribute to E. M. Forster,"
    Times (London), (28 Dec 1968), 15.
    A tribute and a review of Stallybrass's Aspects of
E. M. Forster, which is "very nicely and intelligently done, "
In EMF's public career there has been "too little Hemlock
and bloodletting." The tribute ends with a note that Furbank
is working on "the authorized biography of EMF."

640. Godfrey, Denis. E. M. Forster's Other Kingdom (#9
    in Biography and Criticism edited by A. Norman Jeffares

and R. L. C. Loumer). London: Oliver and Boyd, 1968.

I. Introduction--"The Impact of the Unseen."
Critics have found it inconvenient to pursue EMF's concern with the "unseen." The existence of this "unseen" factor informing the author's work has been, of course, the subject of critical comment but, to this point, there has been no sufficient realization of its essential importance. EMF's "unseen" or "mysticism," his postulation of a transcendent reality, has raised the question of the relationship between that world and this one, the unseen and the seen.

II. The Short Stories. They are, for the most part, fantasies, usually treating an occurrence of a supernatural kind which erupts in the midst of everyday reality. The characters react to it in accord with the degree of their spiritual sensitivity. What counts most in these stories is not the impossible events but the reactions of the characters to them. In some tales, the unseen continues to be manifest, but less open. Nevertheless, the unseen is still basic to these stories and to the novels. In the stories, the unseen becomes a "touchstone" for the judgment of character. Though the novels lead more deeply into human experience they do not, in this respect, go beyond the short stories.

III. Where Angels Fear to Tread. Philip and Miss Abbott are saved by the Italian "unseen," but only because they are capable of harmonizing "the primitive mysticism of the heart with the moral and intellectual achievements of Sawston." Nevertheless, there is something "ultimately unsatisfying" in the means of salvation offered us through these two characters. Obviously, not everyone can embroil himself in Italy to save himself. Is there any other way? EMF addresses himself to this problem in LJ.

IV. The Longest Journey. The novel proposes a theory, through Stephan, that self-knowledge, any advance into self-awareness, is not in fact an advance but a retreat. Stephan, in contrast to all the other characters, is unselfconscious, a creature of instinct. This is the source of his strength. Against the England of the self-conscious has been set the England of instinct, which is sustained by the "mystic emanations of the ancient soil." Rickie represents the former and thus is allowed to go down to defeat.

V. A Room with a View. The novel contains "fewer direct intimations of spiritual forces than either of the first two novels." Nevertheless, the reader never ceases to be made aware of the Italian "presence," and of the issues to which it gives rise. Lucy, whose salvation through Italy and through love is the central theme, is ignorant, almost to the end, of the impulses at work within herself. Yet, she finally senses "deities reconciled" and, in gaining the man she loves, she has gained something for the "whole world." The novel is, perhaps, no more than a second demonstration after WAFT of the "redemptive power of the Italian unseen in impact upon the English character." But the novel does include, with greater definiteness and precision than in WAFT, the confrontations with individuals in league with a source of spiritual malevolence.

    VI. <u>Howards End</u>. EMF's reticence on the subject of the unseen comes to an end with HE. Throughout the book, the conflict with the seen--the outer world of the Wilcoxes-- and the unseen--the inner world of the Schlegels--is basic. It is Margaret's mission to reconcile the two. "Only Connect" is the whole of her sermon. The Schlegels, nevertheless, because they are only half English, may qualify at best for only a limited degree of salvation.

    VII. <u>A Passage to India</u>. In PI, the basic concept of the unseen attained in HE remains substantially unaltered, though the unseen is "less explicitly vouched for." Though explicit phrases such as "the impact of the unseen" are not used; it is nevertheless present at all times. It is to Mrs. Moore, "true successor in almost every respect of Ruth Wilcox," that we must turn for the principal indications of its nature and its mode of operation. PI does not go beyond HE in the unseen, but does develop the concept in depth. This final novel, though superior in many ways to those which preceded it, "represents spiritually a marking time."

    VIII. <u>Conclusions</u>. In EMF the concept of the unseen and its manifestations come to rest in paradox, in positive and negative assertions and implications which cannot be reconciled logically. The existence of the unseen, a transcendent spiritual reality, has not been questioned; on the other hand, entirely contradictory and irreconcilable claims have been made concerning its nature and significance. On the positive side we have been told that it is the means to human salvation; negatively, the unseen proclaims the nothingness of the universe and the futility of human endeavor. No attempt has been made to reconcile this paradox. Instead, the reader has been tacitly and finally required to accept the illogical: a universe that is everything and nothing; meaningful and meaningless. EMF is an artist "poised on a spiritual threshold." He looks back with nostalgia "to a vanishing, unself-conscious spirituality" and "forward ... to a new conscious spirituality ... tentative though destined to evolve and grow." As a thinker, he falls short of himself as an

artist. He cannot go beyond the paradoxes in which he becomes involved.

641. Hall, James. The Lunatic Giant in the Drawing Room:
The British and American Novel Since 1930. Bloomington, Ind. and London: Indiana University Press, 1968.
Index. pp. 21, 27.
Elizabeth Bowen's view about "evolution in manners
and morals, about discontinuity between the structured life ...
and the catch-as-catch-can experience of the city" follows a
diagnosis already made familiar by EMF. Violet in her
House in Paris is her version of his "wise, dying mother."

642. Langbaum, Robert. "A New Look at E. M. Forster,"
Southern Review, IV (Winter 1968), 33-49.
EMF has written two masterpieces, WAFT and PL.
His talent is essentially comic. He is the only one in whom
can be discerned another Jane Austen. He did not continue
to write because, to write like Austen, one has to believe in
one's society.

643. Levine, June Perry. "E. M. Forster's A Passage to
India: Creation and Criticism" Dissertation Abstracts,
XXVIII (1968), 3189A-3190A.
EMF's two trips to India afforded him the raw material for his novel. An analysis of the multiple versions of
many of the novel's events contained in his manuscript, illuminates his intentions in shaping the work. EMF desired
to create a compelling representation of the duality he found
in the universe.

644. Moran, Ronald. " 'Come, Come'; 'Boum, Boum':
'Easy' Rhythms in E. M. Forster's A Passage to India, "
Ball State University Forum, IX (Spring 1968), 3-9.
PI is about the nature of reality, but this paper is
concerned with the "inexplicable" and with the novel's use of
"easy" rhythm which is defined as "repetition plus variation."

644A. Mukherjee, Asinik. "The Split Personality of E. M.
Forster, " Quest (Bombay), LVI (1968), 49-55.

645. Pritchett, V. S. "E. M. Forster at 90, " New York
Times, (29 Dec 1968), Sect. VII, pp. 1-2, 18-19.
When asked why he had written no novels after PI,
EMF replied "I have forgotten how to do it. " There follows a
general review of EMF's life and work.

646. Shahane, V. A., ed. Perspectives on E. M. Forster's

A Passage to India, A Collection of Critical Essays. New
York: Barnes and Noble, 1968.
Introduction. Shahane traces the novel's critical history noting that it was first considered as "sociological expression." With Trilling, the critical emphasis shifted to a
literary and thematic interpretation. Early critics found EMF
"baffling," and later critics found him "difficult to pin down
in words." Since the 20's and 30's there is a distinct change
in the critical assessment of EMF's work. The 30's focuses
upon his art, irony, social comedy, technique. There was a
gradual shift from this position to an examination of the
philosophical aspects of that work.
      I.   White, Gertrude M. A Passage to India: Analy-
sis and Revaluation." see: #313.
      II. Maclean, Hugh. "The Structure of A Passage to
India," see: #297.
      III. Hollingsworth, Kenneth. "A Passage to India:
The Echoes in the Marabar Caves." see: #492.
      IV. Dauner, Louise. "What Happened in the Cave?
Reflections on A Passage to India." see: #454.
      V.   Nierenberg, Edwin. "The Withered Priestess:
Mrs. Moore's Incomplete Passage to India." see: #552.
      VI. Boyle, Ted E. "Adela Quested's Delusion: The
Failure of Rationalism in A Passage to India." see #565.
      VII. McConkey, James, "The Prophetic Novel: A
Passage to India," see: #387 The Novels of E. M. Forster,
"The Prophetic Novel: A Passage to India."
      VIII. Shusterman, David. "The Curious Case of
Dr. Godbole, A Passage to India Re-Examined." see #473.
      IX. Thomson, George H. "Thematic Symbol in
A Passage to India." see: #477.
      X.   Chaudhuri, Nirad C. "Passage to and from
India." see: #316.
      XI. Allen, Glen O. "Structure, Symbol, and
Theme in A Passage to India." see: #333.
      XII. Shahane, V. A. "Symbolism in A Passage to
India: 'Temple'." see: #529.
      XIII. Parry, Bonita. "Passage to More Than India."
see: #587 (XIII).
      XIV. Gransden, K. W. "The Last Movement of the
Symphony." see: #690.

647. Shonfield, Andrew. "Politics of E. M. Forster's India,"
      Encounter, XXX (Jan 1968), 62-69. Reprinted: Dis-
      cussion, XXX (June 1968), 94-96.
      The drama of PI revolves about a "conflict of political
attitudes" and exercised a powerful influence on the thinking of

a whole generation of British liberals.   The theme of the
book is "personal relations."

648.   Spencer, M.   "Hinduism in E. M. Forster's A Pas-
       sage to India," Asian Studies, XXVII (Feb 1968), 281-295.

649.   Stewart, J. I. M.. Joseph Conrad.   New York: Dodd,
       Mead, 1968.   Index.   p. 218.
          Notes that Conrad's Chance suggests EMF's sketches
of upper-middle class life in his novels.

649A.   Thomson, George H.   "E. M. Forster and Howard
        Sturgis," Texas Studies in Literature and Language, X
        (1968), 423-433.
           EMF was impressed by Sturgis's Tim, All That Was
Possible, and Belchamber and was probably influenced by them.

650.   Wakefield, George Potter.   Howards End (E. M. Fors-
       ter).   (in Notes on English Literature Series).   Oxford:
       Basil Blackwell, 1968.
          An analysis of HE in terms of purpose (Chapter I);
method (II); characters (III); and achievement (V).   A critical
evaluation of chapters XIX and XXXVIII is given in IV.

651.   Wall, Stephen.   "Qualities of Forster," New Statesman,
       LXXVI (19 July 1968), 87.
          A review of Kirkpatrick's Bibliography, Brander's
E. M. Forster,   Kelvin's E. M. Forster, and Godfrey's
E. M. Forster's Other Kingdom.   Calls the bibliography "excellent"; Brander's book "amiable, tolerant, chatty, and an
old-fashioned survey which communicates little that we didn't
know before."   Godfrey's volume "has a coherent thesis."
One of the defects of Kelvin's study is that "you could read it
without even guessing that his subject was a delightful man."

651A.   White, Margaret B.   "An Experiment in Criticism,"
        Dissertation Abstracts, XXIX (1968), 1521.
           An application to PI of the critical theories of EMF,
Burke, Bachelard, and Christopher Fry.

                              1969

652.   Arlott, John.   "Forster at the Microphone," Listener,
       LXXXI (Jan 1969), 8-9.
          Discusses EMF's involvement in the BBC overseas
broadcasting program, "English to India."   Notes that he was

the one contributor that "the programme had to have if it was
to command respect in India."

653. Barnes, Clive. "On the Scene," Holiday, XLV (March
      1969), 18.
      A notation that EMF is ninety and that, as a conse-
quence, he has been given the Order of Merit and has had a
book published in his honor, Aspects of E. M. Forster,
which includes "many beautifully written essays." EMF is
"fascinating," but, in one sense, his novels are "period pieces."
He was, however, not just a "good novelist," he was a "great
novelist."

653A. Cahill, Daniel J. "E. M. Forster's The Longest
      Journey and its Critics," Iowa English Yearbook, XV
      (1969), 39-49.

654. Daiches, David. The Present Age in British Literature.
      Bloomington, Ind., and London: Indiana University Press,
      1969. Index. pp. 86, 260-261, 265, 281.
      Essentially a bibliography of EMF's works.

655. Delbaere-Garant, J. " 'Who Shall Inherit England?':
      A Comparison between Howards End, Parades End, and
      Unconditional Surrender," English Studies, L (1969),
      101-105.
      EMF's HE and Waugh's trilogy end in a similar way
yet the significance of the event differs and reveals "divergent
responses to the social transformation of England."

656. "E. M. Forster Gets O.M. on Birthday," Times
      (London), (1 Jan 1969), 2, col. 3.
      EMF was appointed a member of the Order of Merit
on his ninetieth birthday. The gift is a personal one from the
Sovereign. His appointment leaves three remaining vacancies.

657. "E. M. Forster at 90," Times Literary Supplement,
      (2 Jan 1969), 12.
      The unheroic virtues (tolerance, good temper,
sumpathy, personal relationships, pleasure, love) define his
work as they have filled his life. He does not believe in the
impersonality of art. In his novels, his good characters have
his best qualities and the bad are bad because they are "un-
Forsterian," i.e. they "cannot love."

658. Emerson, Gloria. "E. M. Forster, 90, Named by
      Queen to Order of Merit," New York Times (1 Jan 1969),
      2, col. 4.

The Order of Merit, conferred on EMF by Queen
Elizabeth I, 31 Dec 1968, is the highest honor outside of
politics and the ranks of nobility.

659.   Gillen, Francis X.   "The Relationship of Rhetorical
        Control to Meaning in the Novels of Henry James, Vir-
        ginia Woolf, and E. M. Forster," Dissertation Abstracts,
        XXX (1969), 1525A.
        EMF employs "direct narrative comment as his most
frequent means of rhetorical control." His "narrative voice"
provides the "connection" between his realism and his sense of
idealism in HE and PI.

660.   Green, Robert.   "Messrs. Wilcox and Kurtz, Hollow
        Men," Twentieth Century Literature, XIV (Jan 1969), 231-
        239.
        EMF's HE casts light upon a theme that is not na-
tional and insular but international in character.   He shows
very clearly that the characteristics of the Wilcox family
must "mould" the whole future of England because they are
the "country's rulers."   But he also sees that they reach out
beyond England and Europe because they are "Imperialists"
in attitude and action.   HE is, therefore, a novel concerned
with the future of the "whole developed, white world."

661.   Kelvin, Norman.   E. M. Forster.   Carbondale, Illinois:
        Southern Illinois University Press, 1969.
        Preface.   Kelvin finds HE and PI superior to EMF's
other novels.
        I.   Introduction.   The bonds between EMF and the
past have been strengthened increasingly.   Paradoxically,
however, his books remain relevant.   His life, until recently, has been "elusive."   To speak of his themes is to speak
of his loves and beliefs.   There follows a short biography.
        II.   Short Stories and Arctic Summer.   The "shap-
ing influence of EMF's college experience is the first element
in the tales to consider."   Of prime importance is the "felt"
knowledge of Greek myth which EMF acquired as an undergraduate and made vivid by his travels.   He is committed in
the tales to "progressive, ameliorative social thinking," but,
nevertheless, could not see the future "illuminated--clear and
detailed--in the light of a new dawn."
        III.   Where Angels Fear to Tread.   The novel has
received much justifiable praise, but its triumph is only
"partial."   Two themes predominate; characters engaged with
each other are also engaged with culture and history; romance is essential for all of life.   Part of EMF's talent is his

ability to be "explicit without being obvious."

   IV. The Longest Journey. The themes rise out of
Rickie's poetic imagination, Ansell's intellectual search for
truth and his moral action, and Stephen's relation to the earth,
the past, and living people. They also arise out of the negation and denial of truth and goodness on the part of Herbert,
Agnes, and Mrs. Failing. On a broad scale, these themes
are conventional society in early 20th century England, the
meaning and value of England's history and tradition and the
connotations of the quest: "what is reality?" The novel is
filled with "symbolic moments and things." Successful in
some ways, but flawed in others, LJ is a turning point for
EMF. Fantasy and romance have given way to a concept of
the poetic imagination. He has enlarged his vision. Sexuality
is never really reconciled with his fundamental creed:
humanism.

   V. A Room with a View. Special comedy joins with
EMF's attempt to create a realistic love between a man and
a woman. This love is an effort to extend the bonds of his
private view of humanism. His affirmation of humanism,
however, is necessarily defensive because of the social comedy he injects into the novel. There is technical daring in the
book; his characteristic, non-Aristotelian, attitude toward
plot is again in evidence, but this time he goes further. He
permits character to generate plot. This control of plot by
character expresses one of the novel's chief concerns: the
responsibility of the individual to be heroic. He also links
love with two technical aspects: comedy and the power of
character to generate plot. The comic becomes a theme.
It joins love to support "character's successful bid for power
over plot."

   VI. Howards End. The true substance of HE remains "elusive" because EMF "probably put more into the
novel than is concretely delineated." The problem of class
also presents a difficulty because of its central and cons-
ciously contrived role. There are many antitheses in the
novel, between the Schlegel sisters, between Bast and the
Schlegels; Howards End and London; the meanings of Bast's
role; the "Imperialist and the Yeoman"; etc. There are
many kinds of symbols in the novel. His use of glass is important because of the ironic connection. Ernest Schlegel is
closely allied with Mrs. Wilcox in the moral meaning and
structure of the novel, and so is the father of Margaret and
Helen. His activism, idealism and imagination connect with
the "ancestral wisdom of Ruth Wilcox." He proceeds throughout on two levels: social realism and mythic incarnation of
the idea of aristocracy.

VII. A Passage to India. EMF seems to evade
answering the question, "What is human life about?" His
intellect and moral vision do, nevertheless, provide some
answer. In the novel "illusion is a danger to reality" which
is saved when it learns or remembers its own attributes and
learns not "to devour illusion" but accommodates itself to
living side by side with it. The persistence of misunder-
standing is a threat to reality. The echo Mrs. Moore hears
in the cave intimates that "nothing has reality." The conclusion tells us that "time and space are the coordinates of all
phenomena" and perfect friendship "would require the oblitera-
tion of these coordinates." By keeping Aziz and Fielding
apart, their existence is preserved. Imperfect affection
"shores up the reality of the world."

VIII. Literature, the Past and the Present. For
the most part, the style and tone of EMF's essays do not
vary, regardless of the subject. He has always refused to
speak in a "public voice." This facet of his work thwarts
any effort to arrive at a "neat distinction of his aesthetic,
moral, and social interests." Two guiding principles are
necessary to bring together EMF's expository writing: "the
largest categories should be employed, and despite his liberal
arrangement, individual pieces must be expected to cross
boundaries." Central to his literary criticism is Aspects.
His ultimate intention in it is to establish a link between life
and the novel, but he "has not reconciled life to art." It
also contains detailed "confrontations of technical problems."
As a social critic and novelist, he has often been called a
"late Victorian." He knows that he lacks "activism and the
intellectual zest for the process of political intrigue." He is
a humanist and, if the historical development of humanism
resumes and if the world survives, reevaluations of his life
and works will be appropriate, but this will mean that his
faith in mankind will have been vindicated.

662. Lewis, Anthony. "Humanist and Sage: E. M.
       Forster," New York Times, (1 Jan 1969), 2, col. 2.
       As a writer and as a humanist, EMF has always
been the "master of understatement, an enemy of hyperbole."
He describes himself as a "humanist with no belief in religion."

663. McDowell, Frederick P. W. E. M. Forster. New
       York: Twayne, 1969.
       Preface. A brief summary of EMF's life and
career with an indication that there has been a post-war revival of interest in his work. McDowell notes the major

critics, indicating that Trilling's work, though "brilliant,"
is somewhat "reductive" in its analysis and "expeditious" in
judgments. Works by Beer, Crews, Stone, and Thomson are
"authoritative."

    Chronology. Lists major events in EMF's life to
1969.

    Chapter I. E. M. Forster: Writer, Moralist, and
Thinker. 1. Humanism and Cambridge. His humanism had
its origin in many aspects of 18th and 19th century culture.
He was an eclectic, deriving his ideas from the Clapham Sect
and its Utilitarianism, J. S. Mill, etc., as well as those influences to which he was open during his Cambridge years.
2. The "Junction of Mind and Heart." EMF is an advocate
of reason but "recognizes the provenance of intuition." Mankind, he held, is involved in an inner (religious) as well as an
outer (political) struggle. 3. "Only Connect": Life's
Dichotomies. There are two main "diehards" in EMF's
mind: the rational, skeptical, logical and the intuitive, religious, imaginative. These form the basis of the contrasting
humanism depicted in his novels. 4. The Natural World and
Human Tradition. EMF believed in the fecundity of the earth
and its powers of regeneration. He is often an "aggressive"
pagan. 5. "The Mirror to Infinity": Personal Relationships.
He held that personal relationships remain "valid forever"
and that they are the only firm "reality" in a world of violence
and cruelty. 6. "The Glories and the Dangers of Independence": The Individual Versus the Community. EMF held
that egoism with imagination becomes the highest aspect of
life; without imagination it becomes the vilest. He was
against restrictions imposed upon the individual by the community. 7. "This Contradictory and Disquieting World."
The essence of life, EMF believed, eludes definition. It is
somewhat chaotic and haphazard. Reason must be used to
secure internal and external order.

    Chapter II. The Italian Novels and the Short Stories.
1. Midway in Our Life's Journey: Where Angels Fear to
Tread. The novel becomes more "incisive" on each reading.
Its scope is broad. It is a subtle, complex and refreshing
novel. He was, from the first, a "mature artist." 2. A
Sense of Deities Reconciled: A Room with A View. EMF
asserts in the novel the primary role of nature as a
power for redemption. The settings reveal his sensitivity
to peace. There is a similarity between Meredith's Sir
Willoughby Patterne and Cecil, but Lucy seems "small" beside Clara Middleton, her "prototype." 2. Forster's Natural
Supernaturalism: the Tales. His short stories are "delicate" and sometimes self-conscious. Some are patent

allegories, others are "more authentic weldings of the realistic and the supernatural."

Chapter III. The Union of Shadow and Adamant:
The Longest Journey. 1. Rickie Elliot and the Life of the
Imagination. LJ is a "flawed" novel but does have its merits.
Rickie is his most autobiographical character, which accounts
for his imaginative power. His greatest strength and weakness is his romantic imagination. 2. Rickie Elliot: Perceptive and Misguided Humanist. His perceptiveness and
blindness in "close conjunction" make Rickie one of the most
"enigmatic and complex characters in recent literature."
He embodies many of EMF's "humanistic and Christian values." 3. Structure in LJ: The Role of Persons and Places.
The three-fold structure of the novel emphasizes the importance
for Rickie of places and the people who inhabit them. The
work has three "symphony-like" movements or parts. The
pattern is repeated in HE and PI.

Chapter IV. Glimpses of the Diviner Wheels: Howards End. 1. Division and Reconciliation: Structure and
Rhythm in HE. The strength of HE lies in its "subtlety of
organization." It has a "three-part movement" and depends
for unity on parallel scenes, a repetition of incidents, themes,
and symbolic images. By means of these, the novel gains a
clarity of intellectual line and intricacy of design. 2. A
More Inward Light: Forster and Subtle Dialectic. The dialectic brings together the inner world of intellect and culture
and the external world of physical and commercial activity.
3. Technique and Character Portrayal in HE. Bradbury offers the "best discussion of Forster's technique in HE." The
novel is a "remarkable fusion" of social realism and of poetic
symbolism. These permit EMF to comment "universally
upon the dualities of our experience."

Chapter V. A Universe ... Not ... Comprehensible
to Our Minds: A Passage to India. 1. A Novelist of Delicacy
and Resource: Forster as a Comic Moralist. PI is his best
novel. In it his comedy deepens to "achieve a metaphysical
significance mostly latent in his preceding books." 2. The
Double Vision and the Tentative Hindu Synthesis. Though PI
is important for its political and social implications, its main
appeal is esthetic, symbolic, and philosophical. He tried to
indicate the human predicament in a universe incomprehensi-
ble to our minds. His main preoccupation is the "double
vision" which bridges the extremities of existence. He presents polarities and through them the seeming paradoxical
nature of truth. In Hinduism, EMF finds an "encompassing
reality that unifies the world." 3. The Marabar Caves:
"Illusion ... Set Against the Background of Eternity." The

Caves embody the "neutral substratum of the universe and lack positive attributes." As Hinduism takes us beyond "good and evil," the caves exist in a void. 4. A "Bewildering ... Echoing, Contradictory World." The structure of PI illustrates a "paradoxical content." Each section is associated with one of three principal seasons of the Indian year. The motion of PI is not linear, but cyclic. There is a structure of thesis, antithesis, and synthesis, but dialectical opposites are not resolved. 5. Imagery: "Irradiating Nature from Within." The patterns of imagery in PI unify it. The method is symphonic. The imagery produces "irradiations" because it is as evocative as that found in formal poetry. His most compelling images are auditory. There are other images based upon the four elements. These tend to make the work "prophetic." 6. Intelligence Versus Intuition: Forster's Characters. The chief characters are revealed in terms of their reactions to the caves and the Gokul Ashanti festival. Aziz, EMF's "most brilliant" creation, is contradictory and complicated and is the only "exhaustively developed character."

Chapter VI. Unexplored Riches and Unused Methods of Release: Non-fictional Prose and General Estimate. Though his reputation rests upon his novels, EMF's other works are important because of what they reveal about his ideas and intellectual preferences, his personality and attitudes. 1. At a Slight Angle to the Universe: History, Travel and Biography. A discussion of Alex, PP. EMF's "luminous mind" makes "Egypt authentic." In AH and Two, EMF follows the course he pursued in his Alexandria books. His feeling for peace endures in GLD and MT. The latter is "indispensible for what it reveals about EMF. 2. A World of ... Richness and Subtlety: Personal, Political, and Social Commentary. Such commentary is "diffused among Forster's books." His fullest statement of his humanist faith is to be found in "What I Believe." 3. Applying Logic to the Illogical: Literary Criticism. His essays on literature and writers are of great importance. He is best known as a critic for his Aspects. His views are "stimulating." He is excellent on individual books and authors. 4. Beauty at Which a Novelist Should Never Aim: Forster and the Arts of the Novel. If he lacks breadth, he is always "fresh, personal ... and ... often deeply moving."

664. McDowell, Frederick P. W. "Recent Books on
     Forster and on Bloomsbury," English Literature in
     Transition, XII (1969), 135-140.

665. Maskell, Duke. "Style and Symbolism in Howards
      End," Essays in Criticism, XIX (july 1969), 292-308.
          EMF's style "provokes strong reactions." He has
two tones of voice: a "poetic" one which expresses a response to the English countryside and a "conversational"
one used for "self-protective" ironies and "authorial" generali-
zations. Like his metaphors and authorial comments, his
symbols draw attention to themselves. There is something
"uncomfortably self-conscious about them."

665A. Missey, James. "The Connected and the Unconnect-
       ed in Howards End," Wisconsin Studies in Literature, VI
       (1969), 72-89.

665B. Onodera, Ken. "E. M. Forster to Jidai," Eigo
       Seinen (Tokyo), CXV (1969), 80-83.

666. Perrott, Roy. "The Quiet Revolutionary," Observer
      (London), (5 Jan 1969), 21.
          The author attempts to present a guide to EMF who
is an "elusive colt of a dark horse." The article is based
upon Perrott's talks with EMF's friends and with leading
critics.

666A. Ramsaran, J. A. "An Indian Reading of E. M.
       Forster's Classic [PI]," Ibadan Studies in English, I
       (1969), 48-55.

667. "Sir Learie Constantine Made Life Peer," Times
      (London), (1 Jan 1969), 1, col. 4.
          A note to the effect that EMF has been appointed a
member of the Order of Merit. It was made to mark his
90th birthday and was not part of the New Year's honors.

668. Sprott, W. J. H. "The Sage of King's," Manchester
      Guardian, (1 Jan 1969), 8.
          EMF has been a friend as well as a guide to Sprott
who first met him in the 20's. He writes, therefore, of EMF
from a personal point of view. The fascination of EMF's
fiction lies not so much in the stories but in the comments he
makes about his characters and their confrontations. His
belief in the human race is "discriminating."

669. Stallybrass, Oliver, ed. Aspects of E. M. Forster:
      Essays and Recollections Written for his Ninetieth
      Birthday January 1, 1969. London: Edward Arnold,
      1969.

Bowen, Elizabeth, "A Passage to E. M. Forster."
The author first read EMF in 1915. Her passion for his
novels was formed when they were difficult to come by. She
was attracted first by the "lucidity" of his writing. His work
is "immaculately turned out." There is "magic" in the way
the stories are told in Celest. They exert a "magnetism" in
terms of their "place-feeling." The world of his novels is
one of conflict. She somewhat resents the fact that PI is
more popular than HE.

Wilkinson, Patrick. "Forster at King's." King's
College, Cambridge was the "right" college for EMF. He
had come to study Classics, which brought him into contact
with Nathaniel Wedd. He always maintains that it was Wedd
who wielded a "formative" influence upon him. The Greek
settings of some of his stories come from his studies. Other
than this, what he received from his studies is "rather in-
tangible." Rickie, in LJ, is the young EMF; Ansell was
modelled on Alfred Ainsworth. Wilkinson traces EMF's
Cambridge and post-Cambridge days.

Garnett, David. "Forster and Bloomsbury." The
climate of opinion which EMF absorbed from Lowes Dickinson and his friends in The Apostles is "expressed with subtleties" in his novels. Did these people later form the group
which has come to be known as the "Bloomsbury Group?"
Clive Bell denies that the group ever existed. If it did, it
centered about 46 Gordon Square, the house of Clive Bell and
Vanessa Stephen after their marriage. EMF was on its
periphery. The original friendship which brought him to the
group was with Leonard Woolf. Virginia Woolf came to respect
him and depend upon his opinion. It was Leonard who urged
him to complete PI. Lytton Strachey and he became friends
and "shared jokes and sympathetic appreciation of each other's
attitude towards life." His friendship with Roger Fry was
enlarged by their common interest in Mauron. The author
saw most of EMF when he (the author) was a bookseller.

Natwar-Singh, K. "Only Connect ... : Forster
and India." EMF's friends find it as difficult to resist him
as he found it difficult to resist India. He helps Indians in
the "building of the Rainbow bridge" so that they might connect "without bitterness until all men are brothers."

Randall, Alec. "Forster in India." The author became a friend of EMF in 1924, the year of the publication of
PI, and when the foreign office transferred him to Bucharest
in 1931, he invited EMF to visit him. EMF did in 1932; he
met the Nabokov family and was a guest of honor at a dinner
given by the Rumanian P.E.N. Club.

Roerich, William. "Forster and America." The

author met EMF when he (the author) was a corporal in the
U.S. Army (1943). When EMF visited America for his talk
at Harvard, he visited with the author and his family. He
admired Menotti's operas, "The Medium," and "The Tele-
phone," which they saw together. He was also "enchanted"
by Ethel Merman in "Annie Get Your Gun." Roerich continues to describe the remainder of EMF's stay in the U.S.,
and his second visit.

     Sprott, W. J. H. "Forster as a Humanist." EMF
has characterized humanism as having four leading characteristics: curiosity, a free mind, belief in good taste, and
belief in the human race. Despite the negative productions of
the human race, it has two redeeming features: the establishment and the progressive refinement of a standard of
moral values and, secondly, the production of works of art.

     Britten, Benjamin. "Some Notes on Forster and
Music." There is no doubt that EMF is "our most musical
author." He uses music frequently in his novels, e.g. the
locus classicus in HE. In RWV Lucy seems muddled until
she plays the piano. He talks of his own playing in "Co-
ordination." Music is used "superbly in push and action"
towards the end of WAFT. The construction of his novels
often resembles opera. He has written three essays about
music. Britten found the libretto he produced for "Billy
Budd" written in "terse, vivid sentences, with their strong
rhythms melodically inspiring."

     Arlott, John. "Forster and Broadcasting." similar
to: "Forster at the Microphone." see: #652.

     Fagan, B. W. "Forster and His Publishers." see
#637.

     Plomer, William. "Forster as a Friend." The au-
thor was introduced to EMF in 1929 by Leonard and Virginia
Woolf. EMF loaned him his London flat. His friends meant
a great deal to him. He had the quality of bringing out the
qualities of "ordinary" people. His friendship has often been
"creative."

     Stone, Wilfrid. "Forster on Love and Money." He
openly defied the prudery which his class had about money.
He saw it not only as a commercial symbol, but also a count-
er in the transactions of the spirit. In a sense "money is
to EMF what sex is to Lawrence." In his work, the metaphors for love and money are "interchangeable." He held
that for money to be sanctified, it must be used in the ways
of love, but even love must be curtailed. It works in private
life, but not in public life.

     Bradbury, Malcolm. "Two Passages to India:
Forster as Victorian and Modern." EMF is a paradox. He

is and is not a modern. His literary heritage has its roots in English Romanticism and the world of the Victorian upper class. In PI, however, the visionary hope of the former is lost to an "urgent group of ideas about contemporary necessity."

Stallybrass, Oliver. "Forster's 'Wobblings': The Manuscript of PI." The manuscript consists of more than five hundred pages, often with totally unrelated matter on both sides. It consists not only of the "final" draft but also a large number of earlier drafts. There follows an analysis of the manuscript, its difficulties, and comparisons of the final version of passages with earlier versions.

Thomson, George H. "A Forster Miscellany: Thoughts on the Uncollected Writings." Of the 463 items in Kirkpatrick's bibliography, EMF has reprinted 152. He has left uncollected some 310 contributions. At least one third of these deserve to be made into a book. There follows a description of these items.

670. Thomson, George H. "E. M. Forster, Gerald Heard, and Bloomsbury," English Literature in Transition, XII (1969), 87-91.

EMF is "non-commital" as to whether or not he was a member of the Bloomsbury Group. There follows a discussion of EMF's "Bloomsbury, An Early Note: Feb. 1929," published in Pawn, 1956.

671. Watson, Ian. "E. M. Forster: Whimsey and Beyond," Eigo Seinen (Tokyo), CXV (1969), 282-285.

672. Yoneda, Kazuhiko. "Forster to Orwell," Eigo Seinen (Tokyo), CXV (1969), 348-350.

1970

673. Ackerley, J. R. "E. M. Forster: A Personal Memoir," Observer, (14 June 1970), 7.

This article was incorporated into Ackerley's pamphlet. see #674.

674. Ackerley, J. R. E. M. Forster: A Portrait. London: Ian McKelvie, 1970.

The information in this pamphlet was originally printed in "greatly abbreviated" form in The Observer (see: #673). The friendship of the author for EMF was the "closest and most influential" in Ackerley's life. The purpose is

not to write of EMF the novelist, but EMF the man. He
could quickly sense the true character of people. On the
whole he was a silent man. His special ability is to "hear
what people are like." The pamphlet continues in this vein.

675. Anderson, Patrick. "E. M. Forster," Spectator,
    CCXXIV (13 June 1970), 793-794.
      EMF's death "removes the last of those benign
voices which were the product of a love-affair between Cambridge and ancient Greece." His "moral vision shines
through a web of often delicious social comedy."

676. Barger, Evert. "Memories of Morgan," New York
    Times (16 Aug 1970), VII, 2.
      The author's personal memories of EMF. Barger's
father and EMF had been friends at Cambridge.

677. Barnes, Clive. "Theater: 'A Passage to E. M.
    Forster': His Prose is Read with Affection at de Lys,"
    New York Times, (28 Oct 1970), 62, col. 1.
      Produced by the ANTA Matinee Series at the Theatre
de Lys yesterday afternoon [Tuesday, 27 Oct 1970] was a
"dramatic miscellany" from the works of EMF arranged by
William Roerick and Thomas Coley. The reviewer found the
readings "enjoyable perhaps [because] there was always something essentially dramatic about Forster's prose" and "much
of EMF's character comes through." The five readers were
Peggy Wood, Teresa Wright, Robert Dryden, Roerick, and
Coley.

678. Bharati, Blaise M. "The Use of Indian Mythology in
    E. M. Forster's A Passage to India and Hermann
    Hesse's Siddhartha," Dissertation Abstracts International,
    XXX (1970), 3901A.
      The investigations of Heinrich Zimmer, Joseph Camp-
bell, and A. K. Coomarswamy into the myth, art and archi-
tecture of India are used in "clarifying the seemingly ambigu-
ous roles" played by Mrs. Moore and Godbole in PI.

679. Bradbury, Malcolm, ed. A Passage to India: A Case-
    book. London: Macmillan, 1970.
      A collection of reprinted articles grouped about
various aspects of PI.
      Part I: Composition: 1912-24.
      E. M. Forster: "Note on A Passage to India";
P. N. Furbank and F. J. H. Haskell: "An Interview with
E. M. Forster," see: #398; Stallybrass, Oliver: "Forster's

'Wobblings': The Manuscripts of A Passage to India," see:
#669; Virginia Woolf: "A Failure?"
          Part II: Contemporary Reception: 1924
          D. H. Lawrence: "Two Letters"; L. P. Hartley:
"Mr. E. M. Forster's New Novel," see: #45; Ralph Wright:
"A Review"; J. B. Priestley: "A Review."
          Part III: More Recent Studies.
          Peter Burra: "From 'The Novels of E. M. Fors-
ter'," see: #104; Virginia Woolf: "From 'The Novels of
E. M. Forster'," see: #77; Lionel Trilling, "A Passage to
India," see: #189; E. K. Brown: "Rhythm in E. M. Fors-
ter's A Passage to India," see: #247; Reuben A. Brower:
"The Twilight of the Double Vision: Symbol and Irony in
A Passage to India," see: #254; Gertrude M. White: "A
Passage to India: Analysis and Revaluation," see: #313;
James McConkey, "The Prophetic Novel: A Passage to
India," see: #387; Frederick C. Crews: "A Passage to
India," see: #485; John Beer: "The Undying Worm," see:
#480; Frank Kermode: "The One Orderly Product," see:
#494; Malcolm Bradbury: "Two Passages to India: Forster
as Victorian and Modern," see: #669.

680. Brogan, Denis. "A First--Without a Star," Spec-
      tator, CCXXIV (20 June 1970), 818.
          The author first read EMF when he (the author)
was thirteen. PI is "more interesting" than HE. Sometimes
"one feels that EMF was 'tiresome,' but how seldom!"

681. Burgess, Anthony. The Novel Now. New York:
      Pegasus, 1970. Index. pp. 15, 23, 32-33, 36, 113, 154,
      162, 212.
          EMF, though still alive, is not our contemporary.
He can never be accused of writing "too much." His technique is traditional. His themes are best summarized in
the motto to HE, "only connect." Few Anglo-Indian novelists
deny that PI has influenced them profoundly.

682. Daiches, David. A Critical History of English Litera-
      ture, Vol. II. New York: Ronald, 1970. Index. pp.
      1158-1159.
          EMF had "one theme": human relationships. When
he exhausted it on fiction, he stopped writing. Nevertheless, he retained his "symbolic significance ... as the special embodiment of ... the English liberal imagination."

683. Davis, Edward. "E. M. Forster (Died July 1970
      [sic])," Standpunte, XCI (1970), 24-25.

684. Donald, Miles.   "The Critical Forum," Essays in
      Criticism, XX (Jan 1970), 108-109.
            Upholds Maskell's attack on the style of HE but
maintains that Maskell should not "deflate" the reputation of
the other four novels.   The "dead language" of HE is "alive"
in WAFT; the "self-conscious" symbolism of HE is "inlaid
in the whole texture" of PI.

685. "E. M. Forster," New York Times (10 June 1970),
      46, col. 1.
            An obituary-editorial.   EMF exposed "in a quintes-
sential way, the human flaws of hypocrisy and repression."

686. "E. M. Forster Bequest to King's," Times (London),
      (10 November 1970), 1, col. 8.
            A note that EMF has left the bulk of his estate to
his old Cambridge College, King's, upon the death of
W. J. H. Sprott who has the estate in trust until his death.
Piney Copse, Abinger Hammer, Surrey, he leaves to the
National Trust.

687. "E. M. Forster Dies," Times (London) (8 June 1970),
      1, col. 6.
            A note that EMF died of a heart attack early yes-
terday while staying with friends in Coventry.

688. Fielding, K. J.   "1870-1900: Forster and Reaction,"
      Dickensian, LXVI (1970), 85-100.

689. "Forster Dies; Wrote 'A Passage to India'," New York
      Times, (8 June 1970), 1.
            London. 7 June. E. M. Forster, the novelist, died
today in Coventry; he was ninety-one years old and had received the Order of Merit, the highest non-political distinction bestowable by a British Sovereign.

689A. Furbank, P. M.   "Personality of E. M. Forster,"
      Encounter, XXXV (Nov 1970), 61-2.

690. Gransden, K. W.   E. M. Forster. (#13 in Writers
      and Critics Series).   Edinburgh: Oliver and Boyd, 1970.
      Revised edition.
            Preface notes that the present edition is more of a
re-issue than a revised edition.   No major changes have oc-
curred since its first publication in 1962.
            I.   Introduction. To some extent, a parallel exists
between EMF and Gide.   There follows a summary of EMF's

life with a note that, although he was in some way connected with Bloomsbury, it is "not particularly helpful to read his books with the group too much in mind," despite the position of some of his critics. His literary career can be regarded as an "attempt to explore ... criticize and modify the values and attitudes he had learned as a young man." The influence of Butler is detectable. EMF "may have been influenced by Meredith from whom he learned to write elegantly" and "certainly by Jane Austen" from whom he learned the "possibilities of domestic comedy."

Chapter II. Explorations. Some of his short stories belong to the tradition of the 19th century. The point behind all of his stories is the "dangerous" view of reality "passionately" held by the author and offered to the reader in the hope that he, the reader, will prefer it to the "safe" view held by the conventional. He prefers to approach passion obliquely. The working-class Italian becomes the symbol of sexuality and the middle-class Englishmen are not good lovers. Passion, in his work, is to be understood and respected, not celebrated.

Chapter III. Italy. WAFT and RWV are studies of "English middle-class stupidity and hypocrisy" and the "outwardly decorous conventions" into which "Italy erupts with salutary if catastrophic results in WAFT and beneficent ones in RWV." WAFT's plot is "Jamesian," but the central pattern is EMF's and one which he uses throughout his work: "a triangle of the intellect, the body, and the soul." In RWV Italy becomes a "window through which the good life may be perceived." RWV owes more to Jane Austen than any other of his works, yet it is the most "Lawrencian" of his work.

Chapter IV. Portrait of the Artist. LJ is EMF's Way of All Flesh. It has youthful faults and virtues and lacks the "old-maidish touches" which make the two Italian novels very uncharacteristic of a young writer. LJ is Shelleyan and is "epic in structure, symphonic in pattern, and tragic in its implications." Friendship is its theme. Friendship means survival of the real self and freedom; marriage means slavery and death. Sawston is all that is wrong with England, and Cambridge all that is best.

Chapter V. England. HE marks a return to "domesticity" after the passionate romanticism of LJ. It contains his most completely realized character, Margaret. His moral attitudes are modified. It is a prophetic book about the social structure and an analysis of that structure. There is, despite its insights, a sentimental side to his picture of England. There is "over-writing and over-ripeness" in parts. The novel is "one of the last statements of the liberal

enlightenment. "
      Chapter VI. <u>India.</u> PI can be viewed as the "final corrective" to liberal humanism, "an ironical comment on the historically brief, egocentric Western Enlightenment. " Mrs. Moore is an even more inarticulate Mrs. Wilcox. PI is an historical as well as a prophetic book. The novel touches upon truth as a relative element, less important than courtesy. The caves represent man's awareness of a pre-conscious state. In this last novel "he transcended the limitations of the fiction of personal relations. "
      Chapter VII. <u>Afterwards.</u> Two is more rewarding than AH. There is enough material remaining for a third collection of essays. In his essays, EMF reveals that liberalism must "yield to socialism. As a critic he offers a "teatabling of art. " He is far more passionate and more eloquent with moral than purely literary issues. "Tenacity" is the one quality of his which should be emphasized.

691. Hampshire, Stuart. <u>Modern Writers and Other Essays.</u>
     London: Chatto and Windus, 1970.

692. Laws, Frederick, compiler and narrator. "E. M.
     Forster: a Profile."
      A typescript of a broadcast aired 29 July 1970 on the B.B.C. It consists of personal memories of EMF connected by means of a narration of his life involving: W. Plomer, L. Woolf, Proctor, Sprott, Wilkinson, Ackerley, Britten. A copy is deposited in the Berg Collection of the New York Public Library.

693. Levine, J. P. "Analysis of the Manuscript of <u>A Pas-</u>
     <u>sage to India,</u>" <u>Publications of the Modern Language</u>
     <u>Association,</u> LXXXV (March 1970), 284-294. see: #643.

694. Lewis, Anthony. "E. M. Forster Homosexual Novel
     Due, " <u>New York Times</u> (11 Nov 1970), 1, col. 3.
      The manuscript of a novel with a homosexual theme was found among the papers of EMF. The novel, <u>Maurice,</u> was written between 1913 and 1915. It will soon be published. It is expected that the work will throw more light upon EMF's own homosexuality.

695. McDowell, Frederick P. W. "E. M. Forster: An
     Annotated Secondary Bibliography," <u>English Literature in</u>
     <u>Transition,</u> XIII (1970), 89-173.

696. Meyers, Jeffrey. "E. M. Forster and T. E. Law-

rence: A Friendship, " South Atlantic Quarterly, LXIX
(Spring 1970), 205-216.
The real friendship between the two began with
EMF's "long letter of brilliant criticism" of Seven Pillars
of Wisdom. EMF recognized a "masterpiece." The book
helped EMF to "pull himself together and help him finish PI. "
Lawrence praised the scenes in PI at the club following
Adela's accusation, the rooftop conversation of Fielding and
Aziz after the trial, and the orgiastic aspects of the Hindu
festival.

697. Meyers, Jeffrey. " 'Vacant Heart and Hand and Eye':
The Homosexual Theme in A Room with a View, " English
Literature in Transition, XIII (1970), 181-182.

698. Morely, Patricia A. "E. M. Forster's 'Temple':
Eclectic or Visionary, " University of Toronto Quarterly,
XXXIX (1970), 229-241.

698A. "Obituary: Mr. E. M. Forster O. M. , One of the
Most Esteemed English Novelists of His Time, " Times
(London), (8 June 1970), 10, col. 6.
He has been justly described as a "liberal moralist. "
There follows a brief description of his career.

699. Pritchett, V. S. "Obituary, " New Statesman, LXXIX
(12 June 1970), 846.

700. "Private Genius: Radio 3, Talking about E. M.
Forster, " Times (London), (13 July 1970), 5, col. 7.
A review of a "tantalizing but scrappy" discussion of
EMF, broadcast 12 July. It was chaired by Andrew Shonfield,
and included W. H. J. Sprott, EMF's literary executor; Lord
Annan, and K. W. Gransden. The talk covered EMF's homo-
sexuality, the "rhythm" of his fictional output, his dialogue,
his commentary, and his attitudes to politics and political
commitment.

701. Raven, Simon. "The Strangeness of E. M. Forster, "
Spectator, CCXXV (5 Sept 1970), 237.
The author knew EMF when he (the author) was an
undergraduate at King's, 1948-1951. The article describes
EMF's "day to day behaviour" as it appeared to Raven. EMF
seemed to be "bone idle, " which was "odd because, though
seventy, he had a very perceptive and curious mind. " It is
"astonishing how unhelpful he was in any kind of discussion. "
EMF had two fears: "of imposing his own views; and one

(even greater) of committing himself to any view in the first
place." His "practice ... was consonant with his ethical
principles rather than with his aesthetic or personal preferences."

702. Rose, Martial. E. M. Forster (in Literature in Per-
    spective Series). London: Evans Brothers, 1970.
        I. Forster's Life and Work. An account of EMF's
life, family, education, and his liberalism.
        II. Literary Background. Much of EMF's work is
a study of personal relationships. When he examines
critically the work of his contemporaries, he is "generous,
zestful, and appreciative." He is an acute observer. Blake,
William Morris, and T. S. Eliot were among those authors
whose work meant most to him. He revered D. H. Lawrence as a prophet. Though some of his closest friends were
members of the Bloomsbury Group, he is not "swept away
by movements in art or literature."
        III. Fiction I: Short Stories, WAFT, LJ. Most of
his fantasies contrast the physical and the spiritual restrictions of the real world with the freedom and joy of the fantastic. In the stories, the traditionalists accept "inherited
mores and standards ... class patterns of behaviour and
aesthetic criteria." The young, on the other hand, the poets,
"see visions" and challenge accepted values. On the whole
the short stories are "light entertainment" which "thinly
veils" a plea for us to "observe more closely the roots from
which we spring, giving rein to the life of the senses and
the life of the imagination." WAFT is a "tour de force."
Though a first novel it is "not the work of an apprentice but
of a master craftsman." Harriet develops from a flat character when she yields to a "grotesque temptation" to kidnap
Lila's baby. Philip is partly autobiographical. He and Miss
Abbott are "rounded" characters because they act surprising-
ly. WAFT displays the "most delicate artistry." LJ is the
most autobiographical of his novels. Cambridge--friendli-
ness, sensitivity, mutual consideration--is set against Saws-
ton--self-seeking dominance. The three parts chart Rickie's
degeneration. Through the parts, the novel moves from
the philosophy of the existence of objects through the central
section of companions to the assurance of Stephan that the
"guided" future of his race would triumph in England. The
autobiographical elements "obtrude to the detriment of the
aesthetic."
        Chapter IV. Fiction II. RWV, HE. RWV is a
novel in two parts. The first describes the impact of
England on the English in Italy and the second, the impact of

Italy upon the English in England. EMF is more concerned
with contrasting of class and ideological differences than he is
in contrasting places. The novel proposes two ideologies.
The attempt to link them ends in disaster. RWV "trembles
on the verge of an exquisite mythology." If England had a
mythology, Howards End would be personified as a central
character. It is a house of magic and mystery. Like it, the
Wych-elm has an independent existence.

Chapter V. Fiction III. PI. In the novel, a passage to India is a "non-event"; it does not happen. The novel
comprises a complex study of relationships between Englishmen and Indians. The Indians think of the English collectively, out of hatred and fear, and the English act collectively out
of the same emotions. The unity of the Indians is achieved
only through hatred of the English. The passage between
Indian and Indian is as obstructed as between Indian and
British. Rapprochement on a private basis will not solve
India's problems. It is, nevertheless, the only approach
which EMF believes has any efficacy.

Chapter VI. Critical Works. AH, Aspects Two.
Many of the essays in AH "sparkle," but there is "dross" too,
especially in EMF's enthusiasm for "maiden aunts of moderate literary ability." Aspects is "no heavyweight as a work
of scholarship," but is nevertheless "brilliant." Characteristic of Two is that political arguments are frequently il-
luminated by reference to the arts, and evaluation of the arts
rests upon political criteria.

Chapter VII. Biography, GLD. Hill, MT. EMF
wrote GLD because its subject represented a "tried and true
friend" who suggested to EMF "the spirit of independence,
tolerance and progressive thought." Hill is a biography in
the sense that its central concern is with the life and death
of the Maharajah of Dewas State Senior. MT might have been
more engaging if the Thorntons had "better literary taste."

Chapter VIII. Achievement. Essentially a summary
of what critics have said about EMF. In fields other than the
novel, EMF often excels, but without showing the "exquisite
artistry found in his novels." Music and mysticism play a
great part in his work. He has been criticized for being
"spinsterly" in his treatment of sex, but all of his novels are
concerned with it. He thinks highly of plot, poorly of story.
There are rarely any "loose ends" in his work. Maiden
ladies abound in his work, dominant mothers and aunts.
There are very few fathers and uncles. Frequently, he uses
young men with artistic leanings as central figures. It is idle
to arrange his works in order of their merit or to "find his
correct place in the top twenty authors." That he is great

there is no doubt, but he is greater than most think.

703. Rutherford, Andrew. Twentieth Century Interpreta-
     tions of A Passage to India: A Collection of Critical
     Essays. Englewood Cliffs, New Jersey: Prentice-Hall,
     1970.
          All essays have been published previously.

704. Seymour, William Kean. "E. M. Forster: Some
     Observations and a Memory," Contemporary Review,
     CCXVII (Aug 1970), 84-86.
          In his "all-too-brief meetings" with EMF, the author
"gathered" that EMF "admired the novels of D. H. Lawrence."
He proceeds to quote from DHL letters re: PI, John Middleton Murry, and from an essay by JMM.

705. Shepard, Richard. "Fame was Long-Lasting." New
     York Times, (8 June 1970), 1, col. 2.
          EMF was "always perceptive"; he was a "great con-
versationalist because he listened." He was "outspoken on
his likes and dislikes" and "there is evidence that he was
his own severest critic."

706. Stern, Richard. "A Memory of Forster," Nation,
     CCX (29 June 1970), 795-796.
          EMF's discussions made it sound that he felt his
work to be a "piece of antique family silver, brought out
every ten years or so for some special turn in literary
sympathy."

707. Vidler, Alec R. "Remembering E. M. Forster,"
     Christian Century, LXXXVII (22 July 1970), 894.
          Vidler came to know EMF when he (Vidler) was dean
of King's. Despite his anti-clericalism, EMF was very
polite to him. He cared for his private life and personal
relations. He was one of those "non-Christians" who put
the generality of Christians to shame. One thing which re-
pelled him was Christianity's preoccupation with sin and the
cultivation of "holy misery." He was a "gracious and graceful doubter."

708. Wagner, Roland. "Excremental and the Spiritual in
     A Passage to India," Modern Language Quarterly, XXXVII
     (Sept 1970), 359-371.
          EMF's "liberal vision" in PI "cannot be properly
understood without due regard for the mystical yearning that
more than qualifies it--that enters, indeed, into the very

substance of EMF's worldliness."

709. Warner, Rex. E. M. Forster. Revised by John
      Morris. (Writers and Their Work #7). Essex, Eng.:
      Longman Group, 1970.
          The critical material on EMF's five novels is the
      same as in previous editions, though slightly expanded.
          EMF is capable of standing outside of the liberal
      tradition. Though he has influenced many, there are no
      signs in his work of obvious derivations. Nearly all of his
      short stories are "frankly didactic" and much influenced by
      Greek ideas and myths. He believes that natural passions
      and emotions are good and that we would be better if they
      were enjoyed honestly and without shame. The main themes
      of his novels begin to appear in his stories. Most of his
      characters' lives are "muddled." He is an "artist on the
      fringe of social reform."
          Lack of imagination and hypocrisy are the qualities
      satirized in his first four novels. These qualities are re-
      sponsible for the "undeveloped heart," one of the central
      themes in his work. In WAFT we meet most of the themes
      and many of the characters which appear in his other novels.
      There are two contrasting ways of life in the novel. Wit
      and comedy veil fierce passions and there is a search for
      salvation, a balance, an integrity of thought. Sexuality plays
      a large role in the story. He uses a symbolic or allegorical
      method and his writing is poetic, not realistic. Though not
      his best, WAFT is characteristic of his work.
          The main theme of LJ is Rickie's collapse and re-
      emergence into the light under the guidance of Ansell and
      Stephen. The climax is symbolic and violent. Like WAFT,
      it concerns a failed intellectual. RWV is less serious and
      less passionate. It is more like WAFT than like LJ. Again
      there is a struggle between art and life, between a mis-
      understanding of art and a misunderstanding of life. Italy
      again plays an important role and again a symbolic act of
      violence is present.
          The difficulties of reconciling opposites is again pres-
      ent in HE. "Only Connect" is the motto of the novel, but
      the connection comes only through deaths and a triumph of a
      "kind of sexless femininity." The theme of the novel is the
      inner life. HE is developed with the greatest subtlety and
      contains a kind of "massive or pervading symbolism." It is
      also a novel about England's fate. It defies summary. There
      are two great symbols which recur in different forms in PI.
      The first is the wise, elderly woman, and the second,
      music.

Before the publication of PI, EMF produced Alex
and PP. The first is "engaging and provocative" the second
a "slighter affair" but containing one of his most perceptive
essays, that on Cavafy.

Part of PI's success is due to the fact that people
thought of it as a study of Anglo-Indian relations. It is more
than that. It is EMF's most philosophical novel. It poses
the question: "can any faith exist once ... panic and emptiness is admitted?" He does not answer the question. Perhaps its most brilliantly written passage is that which describes the visit to the caves. In PI can be observed those
qualities, eminently heightened, which make his earlier
works memorable.

Aspects reveals a keen and individual mind. It may
not be criticism of the highest order, but it is full of "charm."
Parts of GLD are not satisfactory, but it does give a good
picture of life at Cambridge. MT is of more limited interest. Hill is of value as a source book for PI.

Though his miscellaneous writings are important
and delightful, his reputation will rest upon the five novels.
His message is not entirely liberal. It penetrates "the
boundaries of deep dissatisfaction and despair" but it brings
back "no key to understanding."

710. Whittemore, Reed. "E. M. Forster 1879-1970,"
      New Republic, CLXII (20 June 1970), 28.
            The key to all of EMF's works lies in the epigraph
to HE: "only connect." He was a "triple-threat man," i.e.
a literary craftsman, a profound observer of the social condition, and one of England's greatest moralists.

711. Zimmerman, Paul D. "E. M. Forster, 1879-1970,"
      Newsweek, LXXV (22 June 1970), 84+.
            EMF was "our last great link with Edwardian
England," but "in essential ways he was thoroughly modern."
His melodrama served to "stress the moral ambiguities of
his characters."

AUTHOR INDEX

The following is a listing of authors of articles and books on E. M. Forster. Included also are editors. The numbers after each name refer to the items in the bibliography.

157

TITLE INDEX

Titles of books and pamphlets are in upper case; titles of articles in periodicals, newspapers, and chapters in books are in quotation marks. The numbers given refer to the items in the bibliography in which the title appears. When a group of similar titles are given, they are alphabetized in terms of the order in which they appear in the bibliography.

"Portrait" 24, 227
"Portrait of a Family" 373
"Portrait of a Gentleman" 110
THE PRESENT AGE IN BRITISH LITERATURE 399, 654
"Prince of India" 303
"Private Genius: Radio 3, Talking About E. M. Forster" 700
PRIVATE ROAD 161
"A Private Secretary for the Maharajah" 282
"A Private Voice" 265
"The Problem of Continuity in Three Novels of E. M.
    Forster" 449
THE PROFESSION OF ENGLISH LETTERS 556
"The Prophecy of E. M. Forster" 551

"A Qualified Tribute" 266
"Qualities of Forster" 651
THE QUEST FOR CERTITUDE IN E. M. FORSTER'S
    FICTION 583A
"The Quiet Revolutionary" 666

A RAGE FOR ORDER 236
A READER'S GUIDE TO JOSEPH CONRAD 437
"Readers and Writers" 67
READING MODERN FICTION 385
"Reassessment: Howards End" 334
"Recent Books in Review" 21
"Recent Books: Mr. Forster in India" 305
"Recent Books on Forster and Bloomsbury" 664
RED WINE OF YOUTH: A LIFE OF RUPERT BROOKE
    235
"The Relationship of Rhetorical Control to Meaning in the
    Novels of Henry James, Virginia Woolf, and E. M.
    Forster" 659
"Remembering E. M. Forster" 707
"Revival of E. M. Forster" 194, 195
"Rhythm in E. M. Forster's A Passage to India" 247
"Rhythmic and Symbolic Patterns in A Passage to India 590
"Rites of Passage in A Passage to India" 535
"Ritual Aspects of E. M. Forster's The Longest Journey
    626
A ROOM WITH A VIEW, ADAPTATION FROM THE NOVEL
    BY E. M. FORSTER 269

"The Sage of King's" 668
THE SATIRIC ART OF EVELYN WAUGH 588
"Scenario of a Civilized Mind" 129

INDEX TO
NEWSPAPERS AND PERIODICALS

The following are titles of those newspapers and periodicals for which entries occur in the bibliography. The numbers after each title refer to the items in the bibliography where the title appears.

INDEX TO
REVIEWS OF FORSTER'S WORKS

The following are titles of Forster's works for which reviews
have been annotated in this bibliography. The numbers which
follow each title refer to the items in the bibliography where
the reviews appear.

LIST OF BOOK AND PAMPHLET-LENGTH
STUDIES OF E. M. FORSTER'S
WORKS AND THEIR REVIEWS

The following are titles and authors of book and pamphlet-length studies of E. M. Forster. The first group of numbers which follow each title refers to the items in the bibliography where the titles appear; the second, which follow the word Reviews, indicate the item in the bibliography where the review appears.

Ackerley, J. R. E. M. Forster: A Portrait. 674

Beer, J. R. The Achievement of E. M. Forster. 480;
  Reviews: 496, 505, 509

Bradbury, Malcolm. Forster: A Collection of Critical
  Essays. 587; Reviews: 602

Bradbury, Malcolm. A Passage to India: A Casebook. 679

Brander, Laurence. E. M. Forster: A Critical Study. 635;
  Reviews: 651

Colmer, John. E. M. Forster: A Passage to India. 617A

Crews, Frederick C. E. M. Forster: The Perils of
  Humanism. 485

Gilbert, S. M. E. M. Forster's A Passage to India and
  Howards End. 572

Godfrey, Denis. E. M. Forster's Other Kingdom. 640;
  Reviews: 651

Gransden, K. W. E. M. Forster. 690; Reviews: 496,
  497

Joseph, David I. The Art of Rearrangement: E. M. Forster.
  548; Reviews: 579

Kelvin, Norman. E. M. Forster. 661; Reviews: 651

Kirkpatrick, B. J. A Bibliography of E. M. Forster. 576A;
Reviews: 602, 651

Macaulay, Rose. The Writings of E. M. Forster. 156;
Reviews: 279.

McConkey, James. The Novels of E. M. Forster. 387

MacDowell, Frederick P. W. E. M. Forster. 663

Moore, Harry T. E. M. Forster. 582; Reviews: 602

Mulik, B. R. E. M. Forster's A Passage to India. 465

Natwar-Singh, K. (ed.) E. M. Forster: A Tribute with
Selections from His Writings on India. 550; Reviews:
532, 553, 554, 579

Oliver, H. J. The Art of E. M. Forster. 439; Reviews:
498

Rose, Martial. E. M. Forster. 702

Rutherford, Andrew. Twentieth Century Interpretations of A
Passage to India: A Collection of Critical Essays. 703

Shusterman, David. The Quest for Certitude in E. M.
Forster's Fiction. 583A; Reviews: 602, 633

Stallybrass, Oliver (ed.). Aspects of E. M. Forster: Essays
and Recollections Written for His Ninetieth Birthday January 1, 1969: 669; Reviews: 639

Stone, Wilfred. The Cave and the Mountain. 613; Reviews:
598, 599, 602, 606, 608, 609, 614

Trilling, Lionel. E. M. Forster. 189, 632; Reviews: 182,
184, 186, 188, 191, 192

Wakefield, George Potter. Howards End. 650

Warner, Rex. E. M. Forster. 709

Wilde, Alan. Art and Order: A Study of E. M. Forster. 558

BIBLIOGRAPHIES, DOCTORAL DISSERTATIONS, OBITUARIES, AND DRAMATIZATIONS OF E. M. FORSTER'S NOVELS WITH THEIR REVIEWS

The numbers which follow each item indicate the place in the bibliography where each appears.

BIBLIOGRAPHIES: 98, 383, 399, 400, 407, 418, 452, 489
490, 521, 522, 523, 524, 538, 564, 569, 576A, 582, 586,
612, 654, 669, 695

DOCTORAL DISSERTATIONS: 298, 341, 414, 423, 431, 474,
518, 525, 527, 533, 536, 571, 643, 651A, 659, 678

OBITUARIES: 675, 676, 683, 685, 687, 689, 698, 699, 704,
705, 706, 707, 710, 711

DRAMATIZATIONS AND REVIEWS:

The Sieveking and Cottell dramatization of Howards End: 503

Television dramatization of A Room With a View: 411

The Rau dramatization of a Passage to India: 440, 441, 444,
446, 466, 502, 503, 506, 507, 508, 511

The Hart dramatization of Where Angels Fear to Tread: 513,
514, 602